Managing Open Source Projects

A Wiley Tech Brief

Jan Sandred

Wiley Computer Publishing

John Wiley & Sons, Inc.

NEW YORK · CHICHESTER · WEINHEIM · BRISBANE · SINGAPORE · TORONTO

Publisher: Robert Ipsen

Editor: Cary Sullivan

Assistant Editor: Christina Berry

Managing Editor: Marnie Wielage

New Media Editor: Brian Snapp

Text Design & Composition: Pronto Design, Inc.

Designations used by companies to distinguish their products are often claimed as trademarks. In all instances where John Wiley & Sons, Inc., is aware of a claim, the product names appear in initial capital or ALL CAPITAL LETTERS. Readers, however, should contact the appropriate companies for more complete information regarding trademarks and registration.

This book is printed on acid-free paper. ∞

Published by John Wiley & Sons, Inc.

Published simultaneously in Canada.

This publication is designed to provide accurate and authoritative information in regard to the subject matter covered. It is sold with the understanding that the publisher is not engaged in professional services. If professional advice or other expert assistance is required, the services of a competent professional person should be sought.

Library of Congress Cataloging-in-Publication Data:

Sandred, Jan.
      Managing open source projects : a Wiley tech brief / Jan Sandred.
         p. cm.
      Includes index.
      ISBN 0-471-40396-2 (pbk. : alk. paper)
       1. Computer software--Development. 2. Open source software. I. Title.

QA76.76.D47 S27 2001
005.1'068--dc21

                                                2001017645

Printed in the United States of America.

10 9 8 7 6 5 4 3 2 1

Wiley Tech Brief Series

Other titles in this series:

To my wife Annika

Contents

Acknowledgments

Thanks to:

Johan Hjelm, Ericsson, W3C Advisory Committee (www.wireless-information .net), for the original idea.

Ulf Engström, Etiska Institutet (www.etiskainstitutet.org), for teaching the human aspect.

Karl-König Königsson, Chronologic (www.chronologic.com), for the basics in open source.

Mona Cunningham, Crealog iDS (www.idsuppsala.com), for being an invaluable sounding board.

Bo Gahm, Strategic Management Training (www.smtraining.se), for fresh management theories in business networking and key customer management.

Lars-Olof Landin and Peder Bylin, of Efficient Business Communications, for reminding us that forming relationships and engaging in dialog are still the best competitive marketing tools.

Christina Berry at John Wiley & Sons, Inc., for being a *very* patient editor.

Introduction

Arguably, open source is the twentieth century's only true innovative concept in business, all that is truly new in the *new economy*. All Open source can be defined, basically, as a software developing method. (If the source for a piece of software can be read, redistributed, and modified, it is said to be open; it evolves—it can be improved, adapted, and corrected.) Open source is also referred to—rightly—as the "gift economy," because for many people, open source means, simply, software that is given away for free.

However, those definitions leave out a very important—if not the most important—aspect of open source: that it is also a valid business concept with truly unique characteristics. It is this second aspect that this book addresses: the business opportunities open source provides, and how to manage successful open source projects.

To understand the concept of open source it is necessary to be acquainted with its history. Open source has its roots in a sort of "flower-power, left-wing anarcho-communism" political arena, a far remove from today's multimillion international open source companies, such as Red Hat, Inc. Open source builds on the idea of giving away intellectual property for the benefit of the community—"What is good for the community is good for me."

In the two-plus decades following the May 1968 revolution, the vision of life without interference from the state or the marketplace has inspired numerous community media activists. Consider as one example, the cultural, free radio stations created in the sixties and the seventies in Europe; they refused all funding from state and commercial sources, choosing instead, to rely on donations of both time and money from their supporters. During the late 1970s the punk movement further popularized these attitudes. Although rapidly commercialized, this type of subculture did encourage its members to form their own bands, design their own fashions, and publish their own fanzines.

This participatory ethic continues to shape innovative music and political platforms today. For one, the Association for the Taxation of Financial Transactions for the Aid of Citizens (ATTAC) is an international movement that seeks democratic control of financial markets and their institutions. It was founded in December 1997, based on an idea in an article published in *Le Monde Diplomatique* (www.monde-diplomatique.fr/en/1997/12/leader).

This brings us back to the idea of a gift economy, one that arises from abundance, not scarcity—though abundance should not be interpreted to mean a wealth of material possessions, for gift cultures are active in cultures such as the aboriginal, whose people who live in so-called ecozones, marked by mild climates and abundant food. Abundance of this sort makes "command" relationships difficult to sustain, and renders exchange relationships an almost pointless game. Social status is determined not by what people control, but by what they give away.

With this in mind, it becomes clear that the society of open source programmers, too, have created a gift economy. There is no serious shortage of survival necessities—in this case, mainly time—but also disk space, network bandwidth, and computing power—software is freely shared. In such a situation, the only accurate measure of competitive success is one's reputation among one's peers.

The scientific community has long functioned within a gift economy, albeit from a totally different perspective. Typically, funded by the government or by private donations, scientists aren't required to turn their intellectual work into marketable goods. Rather, scientific results are "marketed" by presenting papers at conferences and by contributing articles to professional publications. Progress in research is forwarded through free distribution of information. In this way, academics earn the respect of their peers through references in public articles. Personal recognition comes from open collaboration with colleagues; rewards come in the form of acknowledgments.

Similarly, because it is not protected by copyright, open source programs can be modified, amended, and improved by anyone with the necessary programming skills. When an individual does make a contribution to a shareware project, the gift of his or her labor is rewarded in the form of recognition within the community of user-developers. Prestige and power of community members are measured by how much they give away.

The Internet was, and continues to be, constructed around this philosophy. The network, originally designed for academics and researchers, has expanded far beyond the universities and laboratories, to the general public. Open source marks another stage in the evolution of the Internet. Today, few question the concept of giving and receiving information without payment. The result of this mind-set is a flexibility and spontaneity heretofore unimagined in the industry. The Apache and Linux programs are two excellent examples, proving that the high-tech gift economy is at the forefront of software development. The impact of such developments is being felt at the highest reaches of the industry. Bill Gates, for example, acknowledges that Microsoft's major competitor in the Web server market is the Apache program.

Unfortunately, because open source is, in part, a political movement, debate on the topic is inevitable. The commercialization—for lack of a better term—of the open source movement has in fact sparked a raging debate among various factions of its advocates, who can be divided between the moralists and the pragmatists.

It is not the intention of this book to delve into this debate; certainly, it does not take a stand one way or the other. To repeat, the purpose of this book is to focus on open source as a *business tool*. Regardless of viewpoint, open source is here to stay. The gift economy must be recognized as an important business factor; that cannot be denied, so the wise position to take is to adapt to the new paradigm, not fight it.

Overview

Open source is about managing people, not tools. Managing an open source project requires different demands on management and leadership. If managed properly, open source can deliver industrial-strength systems that meet users' needs, and offer solutions that are fully extensible and maintainable over long periods of time. Code developed under open source tends to be more consistent and easier to maintain; moreover, errors in software development can be identified and corrected early, thus avoiding massive code rewrites.

Clearly, open source can help firms conduct business more effectively and efficiently, but not without a thorough understanding of this new concept. It was that realization, and the desire to help companies gain that understanding, that led to the writing of this book. For three days in April 1999, while my old friend Ulf Engström and I were visiting another friend, Johan Hjelm, then at the World Wide Web Consortium (W3C), we came up with an idea of how to use this new thing called "open source," to help companies reshape themselves for the new economy. After all, we reasoned, the Internet is not just smart machines, but the people behind them, who, through networks, can combine their intelligence, knowledge, and creativity to engender breakthroughs in economic, technological, as well as social development.

It was also our intention to use the technology ourselves, specifically, to become an experimental workshop for our own ideas, especially that open source is more than technology. We wanted to further develop the concept of open source to create an organization whose environment was one of true cooperation among our partners, and whose collaborators were truly empowered. To achieve this goal, we believe, requires a combination of open source technology, organization, and mentality.

In sum, we believe an "open organization" or a "business network organization" is based on a single, primary, goal: to keep knowledge within the company, regardless how loosely coupled it may be.. Let's face it, today no one can count on any business relationship lasting a lifetime, therefore it is imperative that companies learn to stabilize their knowledgebase, if they are to compete successfully in the new economy.

How This Book Is Organized

The content of *Managing Open Source Projects* has been drawn from my experiences with an open source project—that is, the creation of the company Crealog iDS AB, a change management and communications marketing group. Though the road to this juncture was rough, the knowledge gained has proven invaluable. It is those experiences and that knowledge I share with you in this book.

Managing Open Source Projects is organized in 12 chapters, as follows:

➤ Chapter 1 provides an historical background.

➤ Chapters 2 through 7 explain different business and project management aspects of open source.

➤ Chapters 8 through 10 present some open source tools and suitable methods.

➤ Chapters 11 and 12 offer advice and dare to predict the future.

Managing Open Source Projects is about the consequences of that new technology. More importantly, it is about the new possibilities and opportunities the Internet and open source generate. It is the intent of this book to help business professionals make the right decisions for their particular businesses, and to encourage them to think for themselves. Therefore, this book is not a step-by-step technology guide. Frankly, I don't believe modern business can be built successfully using simple, process-oriented "cookbooks." Rather, I contend, it's only people who learn to think freely who can manage successful businesses.

On the Companion Web Site

Much of the material in *Managing Open Source Projects* is of a time-sensitive nature, so be sure to visit this book's companion Web site, www.wiley.com/compbooks/sandred, for the latest information on this important topic, as well as additional documents too extensive to include in this book, and links to other resources.

An Open Source Primer

There is no such thing as a free lunch.

ROBERT A. HEINLEIN, *THE MOON IS A HARSH MISTRESS*,
PUTNAM PUBLISHING GROUP, 1966

Why do all books start with a history lesson? Old habits? Cheap padding? In this case, to understand what this new phenomenon called *open source* really is, it is necessary to have a thorough background. Frankly, many ideas regarding open source are not new. They originate from a combination of U.S. cold war politics, Flower Power, and a touch of anarchistic and libertarian opinions.

The Birth of the Internet

Without the Internet, open source would not exist. The National Physical Laboratory in Great Britain installed the first experimental network that used the home-brew experimental research predecessor to Internet Protocol (IP) as a communications protocol in 1968. Shortly thereafter, the U.S. Pentagon department *Advanced Research Projects Agency* (ARPA—later changed to DARPA when the word *Defense* was added) founded a much larger and more ambitious networking project.

ARPA

ARPA had its origin in the post-World War II government support for computing and later the cold war. One of the earliest roots was a visionary article in *Atlantic Monthly* by Vannevar Bush, administrative officer in the Eisenhower administration and a prominent MIT researcher, published right after World War II. In the article, he discusses an imaginary collaborative science and computing network, much like the Internet of today.

President Dwight Eisenhower loved the scientific community. He found scientists inspiring. He liked their ideas, their culture, their values, and last but not least their value to the country. Eisenhower surrounded himself with the nation's best scientific minds and was the first president to host a White House dinner specifically to honor scientific and engineering communities. Hundreds of prominent American scientists directly served the Eisenhower administration on various panels.

Under the psychological impact of the Soviet construction of a nuclear weapon defense in the 1950s, the vision of a nation-wide network began to take shape as the U.S. government sought to regularize its technological research and spending. The industrial policy was driven by foreign politics—the cold war—and was to be a fast-response mechanism closely tied to the American President and Secretary of Defense, to ensure that Americans would never again be taken by surprise on the technological frontier. The Soviet launch of the first Sputnik satellite in October 1957 created a period of U.S. national crisis. The public pressure was high on the White House to act. There were several public addresses to reassure the American people and reduce the minor panic the Sputnik launch had caused.

During that time, the U.S. military saw their chances to get higher contributions. The Department of Defense bureaucrats as well as Army, Navy, and Air Force commanders treated Sputnik like the starting point in a new race, opposing each other for the biggest share of governmental research and development spending. The competition sometimes reached absurd heights, but Sputnik launched a golden era for military science and technology.

President Eisenhower's personal experience in the military made him distrustful of the bureaucratic interests in the Pentagon. Therefore new institutions, largely independent of specific military branches, were created. The best known were the National Science Foundation, the *National Aeronautics and Space Administration* (NASA), and ARPA. The president formed ARPA on January 7, 1958, right after the launch of Sputnik II on November 7, 1957.

A key appointment for the predecessor to the Internet came in 1962 when psychologist J. C. R. Licklider was hired to head a behavioral sciences office at ARPA, an office that would evolve under Licklider's two-year directorship into the *Information Processing Techniques Office* (IPTO). That office was later the originator of the Internet.

Licklider was far more than just a computer enthusiast. He touted the pioneering vision that computers were more than just adding machines. This was presented in an era of almost hysterical technology optimism and horror of the communist specter. This was also the golden era of Isaac Asimov's novel *I Robot*, pulp science fiction like *Amazing Stories*, and TV series like *The Twilight Zone*. This was an era when the president made front-page headlines with speeches drawing links between science and defense.

Licklider believed that computers had the potential to act as extensions of the human being, as tools that could amplify the range of human intelligence and expand the reach of our analytical powers. In 1960 he wrote a manifesto for using computers to enhance research collaboration entitled *Man-Computer Symbiosis*. As importantly, Licklider's university background encouraged him to extend ARPA's funding to a range of university projects. One key project was a $3 million per-year grant to encourage the spread of the new invention *time-sharing computing* (a product of the innovative Whirlwind minicomputer at MIT).

Time-sharing computing is the basis for all modern operating systems, making it possible for more than one person to share the same computer and to run different programs at the same time. It is a technological method to give many users interactive access to a computer from individual terminals. The alternative is *batch processing*, where each program is run in sequence in a queue.

ARPA would fund six of the first 12 time-sharing computer systems in the United States, which in turn would help found the whole minicomputer industry in the 1960s, crucial to the development of the Internet over the next decades. It was MIT hackers who largely designed both hardware and software for Digital Equipment's (now Compaq) breakthrough PDP-6 and later PDP-10 time-sharing minicomputers. ARPAnet was primarily a network of cheap time-sharing systems from Digital Equipment.

The demand for a failsafe network grew concurrently with the cold war and the American military's increasing dependence on computers. Between 1960 and 1964 Paul Baran, a researcher at RAND Corporation, wrote 11 papers on the idea of a nation-wide distributed communications system. He proposed how the future American military network should be structured. The idea was to build something that could survive a nuclear attack and was not dependent on a central switch.

ARPA was never interested in building a network to protect national security in the face of a nuclear attack. The project instead embodied the most peaceful of intentions: to link computers at scientific laboratories across the United States, so researchers could share computer resources. The intention had nothing to do with supporting or surviving a war. Eventually ARPA decided to use the distributed and revolutionary ideas from Baran's papers to network its various research outlets around the country.

What Baran envisioned was a network of unmanned switches. His approach was to disassemble the central communication switches and compose the network of many small switches, each connected to several of its neighbors—a fairly straightforward concept.

Baran's second idea was revolutionary: disassemble the messages as well. By dividing each message into message blocks, and making every block contain information about its place in the data stream, you could flood the network with packets taking different paths all over the network, and upon arrival reassemble the message into its original form by a receiving computer.

Baran tried to persuade AT&T to build the system, but they believed that his idea would never work. One should remember that these ideas were presented at a time when all the signals on the telephone network were analog, all switches were central, many manually operated switches were still in use, and you had to order long-distance connection in advance. The telephone network was *circuit-switched* (or *point-to-point*), which means that a communication line was reserved for one call at a time and held open for the duration of that session. Baran envisioned a network of unmanned switches or *nodes* that routed the messages automatically using a "self-learning policy at each node, without the need for a central, and possibly vulnerable, control point."

Interestingly, in a 1965 paper independent of Baran's work, Donald Watts Davies at the British National Physical Laboratory wrote what was essentially Baran's idea, though he called the message blocks *packets* and the technology *packet switching*. He also tried to persuade governmental agencies, in this case the British Post Office, but likewise received stiff resistance.

The technical similarity between Davies' and Baran's work was striking. Their ideas were conceptually identical. They had even chosen the same packet size and data-transmission rate. Both had adaptive routing schemes, though different in detail.

Soon ARPA got hold of both Davies' and Baran's work. At the end of 1967, at an Association of Computing Machinery (ACM) conference in Tennessee, the first paper that described the ARPAnet was presented. By July 1968, a request for proposal was sent out from ARPA to 140 companies interested in building the first nodes, called *Interface Message Processors*.

By the end of 1968, ARPA announced that the contract to build the router had been awarded to Bolt Beranek and Newman (BBN), a small Cambridge-based company made up largely of MIT graduate students and affiliated researchers, including J. C. R. Licklider at various times.

The first computer connected to ARPAnet was a Honeywell (now Unisys) DDP-516. The machine had no hard disk or floppy (the floppy disk hadn't been invented yet), had a core memory of 12 kbyte, and was programmed in assembler by punched paper tape.

The premiere was a year later on October 20, 1969 when the first node in what today is called the Internet, was installed at University of California at Los Angeles (UCLA). The word *LOGIN* was sent from UCLA to node number two at Stanford Research Institute. In December 1969 four nodes were connected: UCLA, Stanford Research Institute, University of Utah, and University of California at Santa Barbara. What would evolve into the Internet had been born.

First Key Internet Technology

The first network protocol was created in 1971 to allow a user at one computer to connect to other computers on the network as if they were local users. This soon evolved into the standard *Transmission Control Protocol* (TCP). In 1972 the *File Transfer Protocol* (FTP) was created, which allowed individual files to be exchanged between computers.

By October 1972, when the ARPAnet was first demonstrated publicly at a conference, there were 29 nodes in the network. At the conference the first ARPAnet user manual was presented, but it would take 22 years before the first book on the Internet was published.

The first international node was installed in Paris in 1972. The ARPAnet was solely used by scientific and military institutes, and only the United States and its allies had access. During this time, two students, Vinton Cerf and Robert Kahn, both original members of the UCLA graduate student group that helped launch the ARPAnet, published the first paper that described the combination of Transmission Control Protocol and the Internet Protocol (TCP/IP). But it wasn't until 1981 that the entire Internet switched to TCP/IP as the main protocol.

In 1976, ARPA hired Cerf, now a Stanford professor, and Kahn, now a BBN manager on the project, to create a system for integrating the ARPAnet with other computer networks. By 1977, they demonstrated that the Internet Protocol (IP) could be used to integrate satellite, packet radio, and the ARPAnet. From this point on, new networks of computers could be easily added to the network.

Unix

In 1981, ARPA funded researchers at UC-Berkeley to include TCP/IP networking protocols into the Unix BSD (Berkeley Software Distribution) operating system. Bill Joy, the lead programmer in the Berkeley Unix effort, created the new version of Unix including the TCP/IP networking protocol. With a minimal licensing fee, Berkeley seeded its Unix version with its Internet protocols throughout the university world, thereby spreading the Internet standards to computers worldwide.

If anything illustrates both the gains from government support of open standards in computing and the dangers from public policy withdrawing from that support, it is the Unix operating system. The computer industry would not exist on its current scale without support of the government institution ARPA and the U.S. Department of Defense. Governmental funding has directly and indirectly nurtured many high-tech companies, projects, and products, including Unix, the Internet, and free software. The Department of Defense became interested in the Unix operating system because of research ties between the defense establishment and many top-level universities, such as MIT and UC-Berkeley, where ARPA subsidized the development work. Sure, the defense bureaucracy had and still has its own issues, but it is not monolithic. Different groups have different needs and systems. All of them have enormous amounts of taxpayers' money invested in incompatible computer systems. My own country Sweden and the European Union are no exceptions.

Unix was created at AT&T research laboratory Bell Labs in the late 1960s. It was the first operating system that was independent of specific hardware. Unix could be ported to different machines, thereby allowing the same program to run on completely different hardware. The source code was widely licensed by AT&T, and in the beginning, mostly to universities.

Unix was especially popular with ARPAnet programmers working on a wide variety of computers, because they needed to create a portable integrated set of software tools for managing the network.

The openness of Unix—it was distributed with the source code—made it possible for anyone to change the system to fit his or her own preferences. Although it was a great benefit for technological development, it was also an administrative disadvantage. During the 1970s Unix developed into a number of variations (including Unix BSD).

Early in the Reagan administration, the military had carte blanche to buy computers, but toward the end, government agencies required lower costs. One way was to bring standardization and compatibility to the prevailing computing chaos.

The key for making Unix nearly universal in corporate and high-end computing in the late 1980s was the decisive action by the U.S. federal government in support of strong Unix standards. The federal government itself was faced with a mess of different computer systems that needed to be networked together.

Unix was growing in popularity and was available on many high-performance systems. Because of ARPA's long-time study and support for Unix, the operating system was uniquely suited to run the ARPAnet. Because of the close ties of the Department of Defense and university researchers (largely fostered by ARPA), the federal government already had an affection for Unix.

The U.S. government looked to find an operating system to which all bidders for government business would be required to conform. The European Union agreed with this concept. In 1986 any computer company that bid on government contracts, U.S. or European, had to offer Unix as the operating system at least as an option for the bid to be considered.

Sun Microsystems: The Network Is the Computer

No single private company benefited more from, and contributed more to, the Unix and Internet standards than Sun Microsystems. The company started in 1982 by selling high-performance Unix-based workstations and servers. Every Sun computer was shipped with Unix, with hardware and software designed to be hooked up to the Internet. Much of the Internet was networked on Sun Unix machines in the 1980s. Sun even copyrighted the phrase "The network is the computer."

Sun dominated the market for workstations that replaced time-sharing minicomputers in the 1980s. Sun was now one of the fastest growing companies in history, making the Fortune 500 list within five years.

The consistent focus on Unix and networking gave Sun a huge advantage in securing one of the large slices of the $500 million, five-year National Security Agency contract then under bid. Sun's and AT&T's version of Unix became the benchmark for selling to the government and university markets, along with many private industry customers who would follow the government's lead in standards.

Open Systems or *open standards* were terms coined in the computer industry in the 1980s, mostly due to Sun Microsystems (even if Hewlett-Packard invented the term). In a computer context *open systems* and *closed systems* mean, respectively, *non-proprietary* and *proprietary*.

Sun's commitment to open standards reflected the company founders' emergence out of the milieu of the ARPAnet. When Stanford students Scott McNealy and Vinod Khlosa teamed up with Andy Bechtolsheim, who had developed a new high-performance computer using off-the-shelf components, it was fitting for them to adopt Unix as the operating system for their new computer, Sun 1 (as in Stanford University Network). But the software and networking standards were missing. Therefore it was natural to bring in as a cofounder Bill Joy, the premiere Unix and ARPAnet programmer at UC-Berkeley.

Commercial versions of Unix were split between various incompatible proprietary versions. Far from being a widely used standard in business, the Sun team had to design a standard and sell the message of open computing to private industry.

They took a number of steps to ensure that the BSD Unix on Sun's computers was seen as a viable standard. Sun gave away the BSD Unix and TCP/IP networking software with every computer they sold, under the Berkeley Software Distribution (BSD) license. The BSD license is in the open source family of licenses and only requires that the copyright holder be referenced in unlimited changes to code (open source licenses are discussed in more detail in Chapter 2, "Open Source in Business Terms").

When Sun developed the *Network File System* (NFS) in 1984, which enhanced network computing by making it possible to share files between different computers, they didn't try to sell it as normal standalone software. Instead, they licensed it to the industry for a nominal licensing fee; but this time the code was not under any open source agreement. However, they published the specifications for the software on the Usenet so that anyone could design an alternative to the NFS file system if they wanted to avoid the license fee. The specification was open, but the software was not.

Another key step toward a universal operating systems standard was made in 1985. Sun approached AT&T and worked out an agreement to merge Sun's Berkeley Unix with AT&T's System V, further enhancing the public view of Sun's Unix as the standard. The convergence effort was an attempt to blend the best of both variants to come up with a unified system, the Unix System V.

That was the trigger for other workstation and corporate computer makers to do a complete turnaround. In 1987 and 1988 every company in the IT industry began promoting their own *open computing* Unix systems—all with the built-in Internet protocols that would set the stage for the commercial explosion of the Internet in the 1990s.

The Shared Ethic

Concurrently with the de-escalation of the cold war, U.S. authorities began looking for someone who could assume the responsibility of running the

ARPAnet. During the late 1970s there were discussions about the possibility of selling the network to a commercial company.

At the same time, more and more universities were hooking up to the ARPAnet, now called the *Internet*. They opposed the commercialization of the network. Also, NSF formally had the responsibility for the operations and were not allowed to run commercial traffic.

The sharing of software was a key part of the success of the Internet. At the universities, paid staff and volunteers both received and provided a continuous stream of free software and constantly improved its functionality. The Internet itself spread across the network nearly instantaneously, without any of the distribution costs of any new software innovation. This "gift" economy allowed new innovations to be quickly tested and to gain a critical mass of users for functions that had not even been envisioned by the creators of the system. This is the key mechanism and the very foundation of open source. Without it open source wouldn't exist.

More and more companies realized the value of the Internet, as it had become an international resource of universities and research centers, and gladly hooked up to the net. Commercial applications that were not necessarily for scientific use began appearing.

By this time military participation on the Net had become marginal. In 1990 the military researchers pulled out and formed their own research network, and the Internet became exclusively a network of universities and civil companies.

The ethic of shared software was called the *hacker ethic* at MIT, especially in the Artificial Intelligence Lab. From a business perspective, free software and open source are essentially about sharing resources and thereby enhancing the development process. The idea of sharing is the very core of the culture of the Internet. Sharing of software is as natural as sharing of recipes.

Neither the term *freeware* nor *open source* existed in the early 1970s, but it was essentially the way software was treated. Anyone from another university or company was freely allowed to port and use any program. Source code was freely distributed, so that anyone could read, change, or take useful parts of it to make a new program.

Ultimately, science is an open source enterprise. The scientific method rests on a process of discovery and justification. For scientific results to be justified they must be replicable, and that is not possible unless the source information is shared: the hypothesis, the test conditions, and the results. The discovery of new inventions can sometimes happen as an isolated occurrence, but for the results to be credible other scientists must examine the results and repeat the tests to validate the results. Science goes forward only if scientists are able to fertilize each other's ideas.

Much early freely-distributed software was games like Decwar and Adventure, but soon more serious software spread the "open" way. The first shared killer application was email.

Email

The earliest email between two computers was sent in 1971. Email as such had existed for a long time, but only between users at the same computer. Not planned as part of its design, email was created as a private hack by BBN engineer Ray Tomlinson in 1972, as a piggyback on FTP.

File Transfer Protocol (FTP) specifies the formatting for files transferred over a network. It was the first application to permit two computers to communicate with each other. Tomlinson wrote a program that could carry a message from one machine and drop it in a file on another using the FTP as a carrier. The problem, though, was to separate the machine user from the machine itself. He needed a punctuation mark and chose the "at" sign (@) on his Model 33 Teletype terminal.

Under the tolerant supervision of ARPA, use of the network for email communication soon surpassed computing resource sharing. Stephen Lukasik, ARPA director from 1971 to 1975, saw the importance of email for long-distance collaboration. He soon began virtually directing ARPA via electronic mail.

Eric Allman, a student at UC-Berkeley, created the program Sendmail to assist network managers in directing and processing the increasing email traffic. Sendmail is still used to direct over three-quarters of Internet email traffic.

Xanadu

The next killer application came from a European research institute. In 1992 Tim Berners-Lee, a programmer at the European nuclear research institute CERN, developed a system based on the concept of hyperlinks, developed by Ted Nelson at Xanadu.

Today, Nelson is Visiting Professor of Environmental Information at the Keio University in Fujisawa, Japan; his discipline is sociology. A self-proclaimed Designer, Generalist, and Contrarian, Nelson's first book was published in

1965; it introduced the concept of hypertext and hypermedia. He is also the man behind *compound document* (an electronic document that embeds various media, such as pixel graphics, vector graphics, video, sound, and so forth), *virtuality*, and *micro payment*. But his best known work is the almost mythological Xanadu project, introduced in 1967. He touted the pioneering vision that computers were media machines, not just calculators. Now, 27 years later, the source code is available at www.udanax.com with an open source license.

Ted Nelson is an anonymous public figure. None of his ideas or visions are widely known, but his importance in the development of the modern IT industry cannot be overestimated. Nelson today directly influences much of the essential software. The most well known are Ray Ozzie's IBM Lotus Notes, Bill Atkinson's Apple HyperCard, and Marc Andreessen's Mosaic, where the designers expressly have acknowledged the deep impression Xanadu had on their products. Berners-Lee wasn't aware of Xanadu when he got his original idea to create the World Wide Web, but he references Nelson in his original proposal.

Xanadu is similar to the World Wide Web, but with built-in mechanisms to manage notes, annotations, revisions, copyrights, and micro payments. Nelson wanted to replace paper with a literary machine that would permit documents to change and track how, and by whom, changes are made. The important difference between information on paper and electronic information in the Internet is that the latter is dynamic. The electronic document is a set of links that is not created until the user accesses the information.

In Xanadu (or Udanax, as the software is called for copyright reasons) all text is mapped in a linear address space. Parallel with the text is a data structure that specifies format and links in the text. This has the advantage of keeping the content uncluttered. In HTML, information about dependencies between different documents is imbedded in the content. Xanadu separates the content from the layout.

In Xanadu all links are two-way, that is, links contain both *go-to* and *come-from* information. You not only know where a link leads, but also its origin. The file system in Xanadu is called *Ent* (after the treelike creatures in Lord of the Rings) and written in Smalltalk and C++.

Berners-Lee needed an electronic system that allowed scientists to easily reference each other's paper in footnotes, without the hassle of searching through many documents. He created the originally text-based *HyperText Markup Language* (HTML) protocol in 1992. Just for fun and to annoy his French colleagues (really!), he baptized it the World Wide Web, which is hard to pronounce with a French accent. It was created on a Next workstation.

It was with the World Wide Web that the Internet became an international top-level affair. In 1994 the first formal email between two heads of States was sent between the then Swedish Prime Minister Carl Bildt and President Bill Clinton.

Mosaic from NCSA

The World Wide Web eventually found its way to another research institute: the National Center for Supercomputing Applications (NCSA). The initial Web browser, Mosaic, was created at the University of Illinois at Champaign-Urbana where NCSA was located. NCSA's 40-member software development group made high-performance information-sharing and collaboration software, but they also had in-depth experience in networking. In 1985 NCSA created Telnet, a software client that allowed people to access and use computers connected to the Internet as if the user were locally based. NCSA had for some time worked to create a graphics-based collaborative tool for sharing documents called Collage, so it was natural for them to create a team to develop a graphics-based version of the HTML protocol created by CERN.

The result was Mosaic, first introduced on the Unix platform in January 1993, with Macintosh and PC versions introduced in August 1993. Copyrighted by the University of Illinois, Mosaic could be downloaded for free by individuals and by companies wishing to use the Internet for internal communications.

However, NCSA did not want to become a help desk for commercial applications. In August 1994, the University of Illinois assigned all future commercial rights of NCSA Mosaic to Spyglass, a local company created by NCSA alumni to commercialize NCSA technology. The goal was for university researchers to continue developing long-term technology and standards to be incorporated into browsers. Spyglass was responsible for licensing the technology to companies as well as for software support.

Workstation and server manufacturer Silicon Graphics CEO, Jim Clark, a veteran from the Unix standards wars, understood the importance of Mosaic and the need to take control of the standardization of this new Internet tool. Clark left his company and met with Marc Andreessen, a member of the Mosaic team.

Netscape Communications was born out of that meeting in April 1994. Clark put up the capital and Andreessen recruited five other Mosaic team members from NCSA to design what they called *Mozilla*, the Mosaic-Killer. The team was working at a frantic pace to create a beast vastly more powerful than Mosaic. The word became the official code name for Navigator. Later the big green dinosaur became an inside joke, then a company mascot, and finally a public symbol.

Clark did what Sun had done in the 1980s: He created a new standard that the company controlled. But unlike Sun, which rode public Unix standards to rapid growth, Netscape began its life with a direct assault on the original government-based standards created by the NCSA.

Netscape included the ability to display text formatting that did not even exist in the HTML standards embedded in the NCSA Mosaic browser. This meant that Web pages designed to work with Netscape would not be readable by all the other Mosaic-based browsers.

Netscape gave away the client (though not under the open source license) and charged for the server software. This would encourage people to use Netscape browsers and would encourage Web designers to pay Netscape for the server software that developed Web pages using their modified standards.

Many companies ignored or weren't aware of what was happening. The most prominent example was Microsoft, which in 1996 with a great hullabaloo launched Microsoft Network, a proprietary network (or more exactly, a CompuServe bulletin board competitor) that was not connected to the Internet.

That same year Bill Gates was surfing for the first time and realized that he had been dead wrong. Microsoft's corporate strategy change is one of the most dramatic shifts in business direction in history. Microsoft Network was completely redesigned to be the Web site MSN.com, and the company developed the browser Internet Explorer free of charge and certainly not under any open source license, in just 18 months.

So in the midst of the Unix war, browser war, and commercial competition, the emergence of open source software came as a surprise. The catalyst was Microsoft, or rather the reaction of Microsoft's monopolistic practices. It is considered, especially by the hacker community, Microsoft's competitors, the Federal Trade Commission, and Attorney General Janet Reno, that Microsoft used a combination of its early alliance with IBM and hardball tactics to build its proprietary operating system monopoly on the desktop. From that base, it is argued that Microsoft extended its proprietary standards into the market for large-scale business computing, formerly the province of mainframes and Unix-based network servers.

While the Internet at first appeared as a danger to Microsoft, the company also saw that success in molding those standards in a proprietary direction could extend the company's control throughout the whole world of corporate computing—again the same tactics that Sun and Netscape used earlier.

Microsoft responded with a combination of in-house software applications and development tools optimized for its proprietary standards, creating an all-pervasive computing environment that promised a one-stop-shop for any corporation. Windows and Microsoft Office might be less innovative than any particular competitor, but the company's very completeness across all sectors of computing would make up for its rigidity. That was seen as an advantage compared to the jungle of Unix standards. The IT industry had divided into a bunch of Unix camps and left customers uncertain that their needs would be met in the fragmented Unix environment. The Microsoft Windows NT solutions on standard PC hardware were also much cheaper than most Unix solutions, which in the end didn't hurt the buying process.

By the beginning of the 1990s the Unix business was competing dangerously against itself. The Unix promise of cross-platform portability got lost in the competition between a dozen various Unix versions. Therefore no one saw Microsoft munching away the Unix market from down under with Windows NT. Microsoft was able to grab a large part of the server market before the Unix vendors even realized what was happening.

By 1997 Microsoft Windows NT Servers were outselling Unix servers. It was clear that in the absence of strong standards and government support for such standards, proprietary models had a clear advantage in yielding market stability, which Microsoft was fast to exploit. Commercial powers controlled software research and development.

Free Software Foundation

In January 1984 one of the original MIT AI Labs hackers, Richard M. Stallman, quit his job at MIT and founded Free Software Foundation. He objected to the increasing commercialization of university software research. Stallman feared that despite the fact that popular Unix standards like Sun's were broadly distributed, they still remained under private ownership and would be used for proprietary advantage, which is what happened by the early 1990s.

Stallman's goal was to develop software for anyone to use at no cost, thereby implicitly helping software research. He started by designing a Unix-compatible operating system, GNU. The name GNU was chosen following a hacker tradition, as a recursive acronym for *GNU's Not Unix*. He chose to make the system compatible with Unix so that it would be portable, and so that Unix users could easily switch to it. The community of GNU programmers and users sought a nonproprietary Unix alternative to escape the Unix standards wars between competing commercial providers. For various reasons, the GNU operating system was delayed, and the work started with a C compiler and the editor GNU Emacs. Also, commercial Unix systems were still expensive, and no one got the source code anyway.

In the underground the hacker community was working with the GNU development tools the same way as in the 1960s and the 1970s, with cheap hardware.

Linux

The history of Linux started the summer of 1990 when Linus Torvalds, a student of technology at the University of Helsingfors in Finland, started hacking on an embryo to an Intel 386 Unix system as a hobby project, frustrated by the expensive and bad alternatives. As Torvalds humbly noted, it was only a personal hobby project, "nothing big and professional."

After a few months he had successfully written a working kernel. Although there was still much to be done, the project drew the attention of curious programmers when Torvalds announced it to a newsgroup on the Internet. In October 1991 he released the source code. Of the first ten people to download Linux, five sent back bug fixes, code improvements, and new features. It was the beginning of what became a global hack, involving millions of lines of code contributed by thousands of programmers. It was the beginning of one of the most spectacular software developments ever seen.

Torvalds' early inspiration was a Unix clone called Minix. Professor Andrew Tanenbaum at Vrije Universitat in Amsterdam, Holland, wrote it for teaching purposes as an enclosure to his textbook *Operating Systems: Design and Implementation* (Prentice-Hall, New Jersey, 1987). It was never intended as a commercial system, and he had sacrificed performance for the clearness of code and some essential features of standard Unix systems. Furthermore it was copyrighted to the author, an act that forbid unauthorized use or modification of the source code without his permission. Nonetheless, its size—small enough to run on a PC—and the availability of source code at no cost struck a chord among students as well as general users. Within two months of its release in 1987 there was a newsgroup, comp.os.minix, with over 40,000 users worldwide.

The first release version 0.01 of Linux contained nothing more than a rudimentary Unix kernel, and it was still hosted by Minix (the kernel could not run without Minix). Moreover, even as Torvalds announced his project to the comp.os.minix newsgroup, he did not intend to make his system portable or, for that matter, as complete as a commercial Unix kernel:

> Hello everybody out there using Minix—I'm doing a (free) operating system (just a hobby, won't be big and professional like gnu) for 386(486) AT clones. This has been brewing since april, and is starting to get ready. I'd like any feedback on things people like/dislike in minix, as my OS resembles it somewhat (same physical layout of the filesystem (due to practical reasons) among other things) [...] I'd like to know what features most people would want. Any suggestions are welcome, but I won't promise I'll implement them :-) Linus (torvalds@kruuna.helsinki.fi).

PS. Yes - it's free of any minix code, and it has a multi-threaded fs. It is NOT portable (uses 386 task switching etc), and it probably never will support anything other than AT-hard disks, as that's all I have :-(

Posted at comp.os.minix August 25, 1991

By October 5, 1991, version 0.02 was able to run the bash shell that provided an interface for sending commands to the kernel, as well as gcc, the GNU C compiler. The source code was also released at this point:

Do you pine for the nice days of Minix-1.1, when men were men and wrote their own device drivers? Are you without a nice project and just dying to cut your teeth on an OS you can try to modify for your needs? Are you finding it frustrating when everything works on Minix? No more all-nighters to get a nifty program working? Then this post might be just for you.

As I mentioned a month ago, I'm working on a free version of a Minix-look-alike for AT-386 computers. It has finally reached the stage where it's even usable (though may not be, depending on what you want), and I am willing to put out the sources for wider distribution [...] This is a program for hackers by a hacker. I've enjoyed doing it, and somebody might enjoy looking at it and even modifying it for their own needs. It is still small enough to understand, use and modify, and I'm looking forward to any comments you might have. I'm also interested in hearing from anybody who has written any of the utilities/library functions for minix. If your efforts are freely distributable (under copyright or even public domain), I'd like to hear from you, so I can add them to the system.

Posted at comp.os.minix October 5, 1991

By the end of the year, when Linux finally became a stand-alone system in version 0.11, more than a hundred people worldwide had joined the Linux newsgroup and mailing list.

The immediate interest was due to the fact that the entire source code was available for free download to anyone who was interested in using and modifying the system. By releasing the source code for free at a very early stage and also updating the releases often, Torvalds quickly found help, support, and feedback from other programmers. Even as the first official version was released in 1994, changes were being made on a daily and weekly basis while Linux continued to mature into a powerful and versatile operating system.

After slightly more than three years, version 1.0 was released in the spring of 1994. It was stable in parity with most commercial Unix systems.

The development of Linux continued at an accelerated pace even after the release of version 1.0, the first official Linux, in 1994. The latest kernel (August 2000) contains more than 3 million lines of code.

Almost a decade after its beginning, the success of Linux is indeed a surprise. Not only has Linux far surpassed the popularity of commercial Unix systems, many also regard Linux as the best brand of Unix. Linux represents the philosophy of Unix—simplicity, portability, and openness. It is the most widely ported system available today, and the only system gaining market share besides Microsoft Windows NT.

A small development team did not develop Linux in the traditional way of both commercial software development and freeware like GNU. Linux was developed by a huge number of volunteers coordinated through the Internet by a project leader. Quality was maintained by the extremely simple technique of releasing frequently and getting feedback from many users.

Today Linux runs on embedded systems to super computers, but originally Linux was targeted toward only one architecture: the Intel 386. The basics were the same as in the 1970s: low-cost development and cheap hardware. But now the exploding Internet—cheap networking—is a new and very important factor.

Linux is neither the first nor the only open source software. Nonetheless, it deserves a special place within the history of open source software. Most important is the size of the Linux project. It is simply unique in the history of software development. The project has involved over 40,000 developers worldwide. Today Linux has an installation base of more than 3 million users worldwide, a figure that took Microsoft twice as long to reach. All the leading hardware and software companies are supporting the system.

Among the very first to note the evolutionary dynamics of the Linux project was Eric Raymond, a long-time hacker of free software. His interest in the Linux project stems from his own amazement at its unconventional development model when it caught his attention in 1993. As he recalls in his essay "The Cathedral and the Bazaar":

> "[the success of] Linux overturned much of what I thought I knew [about software engineering]."

In May 1997, Eric Raymond gave the first speech, "The Cathedral and the Bazaar," at the Linux Congress in Bavaria. It was a milestone in open source. He published the speech, with minor edits, in February 1998 (he changed "free software" to "open source"), and it was finally published as a book in 1999 (O'Reilly & Associates, 1999). Since then, Raymond has studied the dynamics of the Linux open source project. His analysis, summarized in a series of much celebrated essays, is the result of several years of extensive participant observation and his own experimentation with open source projects.

He was like Richard Stallman, concerned about the vulgar commercialization and monopolistic path the software industry had taken. At the conference and soon thereafter he gathered a group of prominent people in the free software community. He wanted to find a way to promote the free software ideas (essentially because he wasn't happy with Microsoft), but he was also concerned that the alternative Free Software Foundation's strong political antibusiness message was keeping the world at large from really appreciating the power of free software.

The group formed itself as the *Open Source Initiative* and largely devised a marketing campaign to explain the concept. They coined the term *open source*. A series of guidelines was crafted to describe software that qualified as open source.

Cathedrals and Bazaars

In January 1998, Netscape unveiled the source code and announced its support for Linux, largely inspired by "The Cathedral and the Bazaar." With Microsoft's proprietary approaches to Internet fast gaining ground, Netscape and soon other actors reluctantly saw their alternative commercial and proprietary standards quickly losing ground. They saw the global open source software model as an opportunity for survival. They would forgo some profits in order to maintain innovation as the priority that could give them an advantage in technology development.

Microsoft had targeted Netscape for destruction. As we will see, the methods were considered dubious and later led to an antitrust lawsuit. For Netscape the issue was less about browser-related income than about changing the playing field for the much more valuable server business.

The decision of Netscape to give away the browser under the Mozilla Organization and the Mozilla Public License shouldn't have come as a surprise, but the release of the source code really stunned the industry. It hit the headlines of leading business newspapers around the world; even the open source community was surprised at the move. Never before had a major software company opened its proprietary code. The body of Communicator source code at Netscape was called *Mozilla*. Now the name came into use as the generic term referring to the open source Web browsers derived from the source code of Netscape Navigator.

It is interesting to note that Netscape was beaten by their own original strategy, to bend the protocols away into proprietary channels. Mozilla was once targeted toward Mosaic. Now Microsoft Internet Explorer was beating Netscape Communicator with the same tactics.

After months of internal discussion at Netscape about whether to release the binary for free, critical mass was reached in the decision to free the source in an unbelievably fast 24 hours, a move without parallel in the industry. As a journalist with 15 years' experience in the IT industry, I have never experienced such a radical and revolutionary move by any commercial company. It took Microsoft 18 months to change its business strategy to be based on the Internet—and that is considered very fast.

Netscape had a lot to do to make the source code ready for publicity. One of the largest issues was how to handle all the third-party modules included in the browser. Netscape Communicator contained over 75 third-party modules in its source, and all of the code owners needed to be approached. Each third-party company had a choice of either removing or replacing their code or shipping it as open source code along with Mozilla. To complicate matters, many of the third-party contracts were unique and ran for different lengths of time. And not only did the inclusion or exclusion of each third-party code have to be resolved, all comments had to be taken out of the code as well.

Parallel to the code cleanup was the license effort. A group of open source celebrities, including Linus Torvalds and Eric Raymond, was invited. The team scrutinized the GNU General Public License, the GNU Library General Public License (LGPL), and the Berkeley Software Distribution license. After a month of research and discussion at meetings, the team decided that a completely new license had to be crafted for this unique situation.

The team came up with the Netscape Public License (NPL), a compromise between promoting free source development by commercial enterprises and protecting free source developers. The license itself was developed according to the principle of open source peer review.

When the first draft of the NPL was complete, it was beta-tested publicly according to the same principle. On March 5, 1998, a draft was posted in a new newsgroup called netscape.public.mozilla.license, with a request for comment. Parts of the draft got rave criticism.

On March 21, 1998, a revision was posted. The reaction was perplexed: "I told them it was awful and they listened! I can't believe it!"

No one expected that a big commercial company would make this move. First the move to open source, then to really listen to users. The open source community realized that this was a true open source project as the discussions guided the process, rather than providing commentary on its results. The result was the release of the Mozilla Public License (MozPL).

It was decided that all of the source code should be released under the first NPL and all modifications to that code must be released under the NPL. New code on the other hand should be released under the revised MozPL or any other compatible license. New files that do not contain any of the original code or subsequent modified code are not considered modifications and are released under the MozPL or any other compatible license.

All Netscape open source projects were placed in Mozilla.org. The goal was to act as the coordinator for the software, like Linus Torvalds' veto role in Linux, that is, to decide what code is accepted and what is not.

The separate company Netscape Product Development's purpose was to ship Netscape products based on the Mozilla code.

On March 31, 1998, the Navigator source code was released as Mozilla. Within hours, fixes and enhancements began pouring in off the Net. That was the starting point for an avalanche of other announcements from other commercial companies adopting the open source movement.

Others Follow Netscape's Example

On May 11, 1998, Corel Corporation announced a plan to port WordPerfect and its other office software to Linux. On May 28, 1998, Sun Microsystems and Adaptec joined Linux International—the first two large established OS and hardware vendors to do so.

The real breakthrough for open source software came on June 22, 1998, when IBM announced that it would sell and support the open source Webserver Apache as part of its WebSphere suite. On August 10, 1998, Sun Microsystems, clearly feeling the pressure from open source, made its Unix operating system Solaris available under a free license to individual users, and to educational, nonprofit, and research institutions.

The most popular Web server on the Internet is neither Netscape nor Microsoft's Internet Information Server, but rather a free, open source server called Apache.

After NCSA developed its Mosaic browser software and its original server software, the institute, as part of government privatization, ceased to update its software. Instead, a disillusioned group of hackers, some at universities and some in private business, began collaborating in 1995 to privately update the NCSA server in the Apache project (as in *a software patch*). Most of the programmers participated for the fun of it, others for political reasons to protest against the commercialization of the Net, and still others because they were dependent on the software but couldn't afford a commercial server.

The result was overwhelming. (After all, it shouldn't come as a surprise. The software is free of charge as long as you manage the installation, service, and support yourself.) Apache is used in 44 percent of Internet sites, compared to

16 percent that uses Microsoft IIS and 12 percent using Netscape's Server. And the list of sites using Apache includes McDonalds, Yahoo, CBS, the FBI, and IBM. The latter passed over its own Lotus Domino server in favor of Apache when it put its Big Blue vs. Gary Kasparov chess match on the Internet.

In the last week of October 1998, a confidential Microsoft memorandum (www.opensource.org/halloween) on Redmond's strategy against Linux and open source software was leaked to Open Source Initiative. The memo was formulated in a rather hostile style.

Eric Raymond of Open Source Initiative annotated the memorandum with explanation and commentary over Halloween weekend and released it to the national press as the *Halloween Document*. The memorandum applied to open source software in general and assessed the potential destructive power of open source software, suggesting means by which Microsoft could combat this threat.

The memo made headlines. The first document contained references to a second memorandum specifically on Linux and Apache. Within days, copies of the second memo were made public. It made even more headlines and started a week-long furor in the media.

The memos were originally distributed within Microsoft on August 11, 1998. It is important to note that these memos never were an official statement by Microsoft, but were intended to stimulate an internal discussion on the open source model and the operating system industry. It is also important to note that these memos represent an engineer's individual assessment of the market at one point in time.

However, the press took the fierce tone in the document as a grant for Microsoft's plans for dirty tricks against Linux and other open source projects. The hacker community took it as proof of the evilness of the capitalist software industry. Also, the timing was bad—Microsoft had just been prosecuted in the antitrust trial.

Microsoft first ignored the documents, then denied their existence. The huge press coverage forced Microsoft to acknowledge their authenticity but officials said the documents were confidential company information that was unauthorized or unintentionally released. Finally, they ate humble pie and Ed Muth, Enterprise Marketing Group Manager, Microsoft, commented on the content:

> Linux is a competitor on the client and the server. My analysis is that Linux is a material competitor in the lower-performance end of the general purpose server industry and the small to medium-sized ISP industry. It is important to recognize that Linux, beyond competing with Microsoft, is also, and perhaps even more frequently, an alternative or competitor to other versions of UNIX.

The operating system industry is characterized today by vigorous competition. This competition, of which Linux is only a part, exists at the technology level as well as in terms of business models, applications, channels and alliances.

To better serve customers, Microsoft needs to innovate above standard protocols. By innovating above the base protocol, we are able to deliver advanced functionality to users. An example of this is adding transactional support for DTC over HTTP. This would be a value-add and would in no way break the standard or undermine the concept of standards, of which Microsoft is a significant supporter. Yet it would allow us to solve a class of problems in value chain integration for our Web-based customers that are not solved by any public standard today. Microsoft recognizes that customers are not served by implementations that are different without adding value; we therefore support standards as the foundation on which further innovation can be based.

www.microsoft.com/NTServer/nts/news/mwarv/linuxresp.asp

Today, open source is widely accepted as a professional business model. It is considered a valid alternative to the Windows NT Server. Oracle, IBM, Cisco, Hewlett-Packard, Intel, Sun, and all the other major providers of enterprise solutions have embraced Linux or ported their software to Linux.

Summary

The history of the Internet is based on the culture of the free sharing of information. This influences the business model of open source we now see emerging and transforming the whole industry. Academic research is built on cooperation, not competition. Open source is also built on cooperation.

The sharing of software was a key part of the success of the Internet. Both paid staff and volunteers at the universities got and provided free software, and constantly improved its functionality, without any distribution costs. This gift economy allowed new innovations to be quickly tested and improved.

This is the key mechanism and the very foundation of open source, but it conflicts with the economical interest of the software and media industry. A large part of the modern industry lies in protecting intellectual property through patents, copyright, and trademarks. Open source fundamentally changes this paradigm.

Open Source in Business Terms

....

Thou shalt also ponder upon to never let a day pass without learning something useful, if you want to be called well-advised. And do not imitate them, that dislike when others tell them or teach them something that they could have use for to learn. Let it be as much a great honour to take as to give learning, if you want to be called wise.

KONUNGS SKUGGSJÁ, *THE KING'S MIRROR*, PUBLISHED 1240 IN REYKJAVÍK.

At first glance, the open source development concept seems strange: Get a bunch of fragmented and scattered volunteer programmers, and make them work in harmony developing and debugging software toward a common goal, in spite of the fact that they may never meet, may never make a dime for their efforts, and must freely distribute the source code they create.

Do volunteer developers write reliable software? What kind of business is it if the code is free?

First answer: Yes.

Second answer: Lucrative.

The way to get high reliability results in engineering and science is by institutionalizing peer review. Physicists do not hide their experimental plans from each other. Instead, they skeptically check each other's works to ensure quality. Engineers do not build dams or suspension bridges without first having the blueprints sanity-checked by other engineers independent of the original design group.

Historically, the software industry has been unreliable. Crashes, hangs, and lost data are still commonplace. Independent peer review of source code is very uncommon. Instead, quality is ensured by different software development methods.

These facts seem unconnected until you look at the infrastructure of the Internet. All the Internet's core software is open source, and the reliability of the network is good to say the least. The Internet is multiplatform, heterogeneous, and global, and it has remained essentially backward compatible through 30 years and several generations of technology. The pattern is simple and compelling: Open source software is developed with peer review and has high reliability.

A Gift Economy

Within the developed world, most politicians and corporate leaders believe that the future of capitalism lies in the trade of information. The purpose of protecting intellectual property is to stop users from having access to the source of knowledge. Profit is generated when someone exploits scarcity of market information. But if the creators of information can reproduce it cheaply, others can copy it cheaply. Therefore, over the last few decades intellectual property rights have been steadily tightened through patents, copyright, and trademarks.

However, this conflicts with scientific needs. It is well-known that a free flow of information promotes progress, growth, and production. Secrecy prevents people from helping each other to solve common problems. In contrast, the technical and social structure of the Internet has developed to encourage open cooperation among its participants.

All academic research is built on open source cooperation; that is, information is given away free. The reward is fame and the awareness that others improve one's own result, which can be used again.

Within the scientific community, the "gift economy" has long been the primary method of reward. As scientists' wages are funded by the state or by donations, they don't have to turn their intellectual work directly into marketable commodities. Instead, research results are publicized by presenting papers at conferences and by contributing articles to professional journals.

The collaboration of many different academics who are located worldwide is made possible through the free distribution of information. Despite their anonymity, scientists acquire intellectual respect from each other through citations in articles and other forms of public acknowledgment. The reference list is as important as a degree or salary.

Scientists, therefore, can only obtain personal recognition for their individual efforts by openly collaborating with each other. Individual value for scientists is measured by the number of scientific journal articles published and articles referred.

Although research is being increasingly commercialized, the giving away of findings remains the most efficient method of solving common problems within a particular scientific discipline. Tim Berners-Lee specifically designed the World Wide Web for this purpose. From its earliest days, the free exchange of information has therefore been firmly embedded within the technologies and social protocols of the Internet.

The notion that *information wants to be free* comes from computer scientists who lived within the academic gift economy. Therefore, the founders of the Internet never bothered to protect intellectual property within computer-mediated communications. They developed these new technologies to advance their careers by giving away intellectual property. They tried eliminating all barriers to the distribution of scientific research instead of enforcing copyright.

In Commercial Terms

Does this gift economy work in the commercial world? IBM and Apple are two interesting cases. IBM made its Java compiler, Jikes, and email program, Secure Mailer, open source. Apple made the two lowest levels of its operating system, MacOS X, open source.

It makes business sense for IBM to participate in the open source movement. It is not a question of taking over the movement, but a question of eliminating the fear from executives and workers, and educating the company about open source. The participation had to be balanced against the business design.

Commercially, participation in open source is a way of controlling, or at least having an influence on, standards work. IBM got involved because it was the most efficient way to have a finger in the standards pie. When companies communicate about creating a standards base, the market grows and everybody benefits. And right now, it is about the growth of Internet-mediated open standards. For IBM, open source development is an effective way to set standards because the portability of the code increases.

Interestingly, in the consumer industry all corporations have always cooperated around standards. The standards are developed by formal standards committees and open for any one to use for an administrative fee. In the IT industry many standards are de facto, which means that someone owns them and licenses them for a fee.

In the 1960s and 1970s, all IBM products were delivered with source code included. IBM stopped the habit when mainframe vendors like Amdahl started to compete with IBM-compatible mainframes. Now we are back to square one. Development is suddenly collaborative, which is a new and different way of developing software. (Interestingly enough, during the end of the 1970s, IBM was forced by the U.S. Supreme Court to separate their mainframe hardware business from their software business, and was not allowed to bundle their software with their hardware, much like the Microsoft case today.)

Comparing the new business model of software development to the traditional model is similar to comparing the client-server development model to the mainframe model: if a company can understand the mechanisms and understand how to utilize them and make money, it is an opportunity and not a threat. Open source unleashes programming talent, and the time to market for products is compressed.

When doing business with an open source corporation, whom do you do business with? According to Marx, you pay people for their work. People should be paid to be productive, and the economy should be somewhere else. Because there is no cost for distribution, the economy is somewhere else.

In an open source project, anyone can participate. They can communicate and cooperate. IBM participates in open source projects as a worker bee. They are currently involved in 60 different projects, not necessarily on the core team. The ones they have joined, they have joined as peers.

But participating in open source development does not mean that companies do not take out patents on the technologies they develop. What has not been resolved is under which circumstances companies assert these patents and what terms apply.

Licenses, Licenses, Licenses

NOTE Please visit the companion Web site at www.wiley.com/compbooks/sandred for the full text of the licenses discussed in this section.

When Netscape decided to release their source code Mozilla, the big question was the license effort. Netscape didn't want to draft new licenses. But to accommodate all of the third-party code in the browser and to make the project work on a corporate level, it was a necessity.

The main question was if any of the existing licenses would work with the open code. Until this point, no existing proprietary software had ever been released under a free source license.

A group of open source community leaders, including Linus Torvalds, Eric Raymond, and Tim O'Reilly, was invited to visit the Netscape Mountain View campus to act as a sounding board for ideas. They spoke with audiences of executives, attorneys, and programmers about what to expect, and met with small groups to talk about some of the issues they were likely to face. They spent a great deal of time with the Netscape legal team discussing the existing licenses.

There are several open source licenses, with various degrees of freedom and objectives: the GNU General Public License, the GNU Library General Public License, and the BSD license. The Netscape team scrutinized these existing licensing agreements, trying to determine whether one of them would work for Mozilla.

Netscape's existing code base presented unique circumstances. None of these licenses had been used for old code. One of the most difficult issues was the private licensing agreements that governed many of the third-party components used in the code. The new open license needed to create an environment in which these and other new commercial developers could contribute their code to Mozilla while still protecting their business interests.

The more permissive BSD license, which only requires that the copyright holder be referenced in unlimited changes to code, was insufficient for Mozilla development. There is no guarantee in the BSD license that modifications are returned to the open source community. This point alone was a big issue because it is crucial to the long-term viability of open source development efforts.

The most well known license, GNU General Public License (GPL), from the Free Software Foundation, was also insufficient. When applied to an original piece of code, any other code that goes into the original must also be covered under the GPL. This aspect made it inapplicable for commercial software developers. For instance, the GPL requires that third-party components compiled into branded versions of Communicator also must be released under the GPL, something outside of Netscape's reach, as Netscape does not control these third parties. Netscape itself also uses a portion of the Communicator code in its other "closed source" products such as servers. Since Netscape has no immediate plans to release that source code, the GPL would present the same problem for Netscape as for other companies.

The team realized that a new license had to be crafted for this unique situation. The Netscape Public License (NPL) was an attempt to strike a compromise between promoting free source development by commercial enterprises and protecting free source developers. The process of fashioning a next-generation open source license took over a month.

The development of the NPL was beta-tested publicly. On March 5, 1998, a first draft was posted in a new newsgroup called netscape.public.mozilla .license, and a request was made for public comment and immediately received response. The community objected that the portion of the beta license that considered Netscape's own interest, a compromise in the first place, would not work.

Netscape did not make a distinction between bug fixes and new code. A bug fix (a small modification to a program) is quite different from adding a new feature to a program. Most people feel comfortable with giving away a bug fix, and the value of making a contribution is its own reward. But new code is a different story. A developer who has done a lot of new work doesn't want to see anyone else use it to make money.

People suddenly realized that this crafting of legal argument in an open forum, which had nothing to do with programming, was a true open source project. The discussions in the newsgroups were helping to guide the process, rather than providing commentary on its results.

The license team went back to the drawing board. They sought a solution that would allow Netscape to balance the goals of engaging free source developers while continuing to meet the company's business objectives. The result was the release of the Mozilla Public License (MozPL) that excluded the amendments granting Netscape additional rights.

Netscape decided to release all of the source code on March 31, 1998 under the NPL. All modifications to that code must also be released under the NPL. Changes to files contained in the source code are considered modifications and are covered by the NPL.

New code developed can be released under the MozPL or any other compatible license. New files that do not contain any of the original code or subsequent modified code are not considered modifications and are not covered by the NPL. This resulting code can be covered by any compatible license.

The GPL is not compatible with the Netscape Public License or the Mozilla Public License. The GPL is by design incompatible with all other licenses because it prohibits the addition of any restrictions or further permissions to its boundaries. All code developed to work with GPL software must in turn be covered by the GPL. The GPL insists that when you distribute code covered under its terms, it must be complete and entire. The NPL does not have this condition.

The legal infrastructure in open source licensing is a big barrier to corporate cooperation. It was considered important to create an atmosphere that made it possible for large, profit-making organizations to understand and adopt this model and participate in the movement.

IBM Public License Version 1.0 for the Jikes Compiler resembles NPL. The source code is licensed to the user, but IBM reserves all of the rights. If a copyright dispute should occur, IBM reserves the right to withdraw all licenses. In that case, a product that uses Jikes or Secure Mailer code must be destroyed.

Apple uses the same principle in its MacOS X license. But a user of MacOS X code is required to notify Apple via a special Web page if the software is distributed.

The IBM and Apple licenses are pseudo-open source as they publish the open source collectively. Open source states that source code distribution must be unrestricted.

An Open Economy

The *Open Source Initiative* (OSI) publishes standards for open source licenses. The organization has created a certification mark, *OSI Certified*, to be applied only to software that is distributed under an open source license that meets criteria set by the OSI as representative of the open software community. This certification mark informs users of that software that the license complies with the intent of the open source definition.

The important point about open source or free software is that you are allowed to modify the source code without restrictions. You are allowed to customize a program to your own needs or get rid of problems, and pass the modified program on under the same conditions that applied to the original version. Various licenses attempt to ensure this. The most liberal one is the BSD license, which is used for the free BSD Unix versions and the Apache Web server. It simply says that anyone can do what they want with it. The only service in return is to add credits for the work done by the original developers. A BSD license does not require this software to be re-released.

In contrast to this, Free Software Foundation's GNU General Public License (GPL) insists that programs based on GPL source codes, or even containing parts of such sources, be released under GPL. This regulation is called copy-left, and makes sure the code remains free.

Apart from the question of how to preserve the programs' free nature, these licenses also regulate U.S. liabilities. There is a dispute as to whether this is possible under European legislation. In the United States, it is possible to release one's hold of the ownership and hand over the ownership to the *public domain*, a legal concept that does not have any equivalent in Europe. In Europe all information is copyright protected by common European law, even if the originator disclaims the ownership. Without that regulation, virus programmers couldn't be held responsible. In Europe someone is always the owner of an intellectual property, and the responsibility of maintenance of the property goes hand-in-hand with the ownership.

The main advantage of free software is its openness: If a program is released as open source (this also includes algorithms, interfaces, or the protocols used, for example), it enables other developers to take it from there.

Eric S. Raymond has formulated 19 lessons in his manifesto of the Open Source Movement, the essay "The Cathedral and the Bazaar" (O'Reilly & Associates, 1999, www.firstmonday.org/issues/issue3_3/raymond/index.html):

1. Every good work of software starts by scratching a developer's personal itch.

2. Good programmers know what to write. Great ones know what to rewrite (and reuse).

3. "Plan to throw one away; you will, anyhow." (Fred Brooks, *The Mythical Man-Month*, Chapter 11), (Addison-Wesley, 1986).

4. If you have the right attitude, interesting problems will find you.

5. When you lose interest in a program, your last duty to it is to hand it off to a competent successor.

6. Treating your users as co-developers is your least-hassle route to rapid code improvement and effective debugging.

7. Release early. Release often. And listen to your customers.

8. Given a large enough beta-tester and co-developer base, almost every problem will be characterized quickly and the fix obvious to someone.

9. Smart data structures and dumb code works a lot better than the other way around.

10. If you treat your beta-testers as if they're your most valuable resource, they will respond by becoming your most valuable resource.

11. The next best thing to having good ideas is recognizing good ideas from your users. Sometimes the latter is better.

12. Often, the most striking and innovative solutions come from realizing that your concept of the problem was wrong.

13. Perfection (in design) is achieved not when there is nothing more to add, but rather when there is nothing more to take away.

14. Any tool should be useful in the expected way, but a truly great tool lends itself to uses you never expected.

15. When writing gateway software of any kind, take pains to disturb the data stream as little as possible—and never throw away information unless the recipient forces you to!

16. When your language is nowhere near Turing-complete, syntactic sugar can be your friend.

17. A security system is only as secure as its secret. Beware of pseudo-secrets.

18. To solve an interesting problem, start by finding a problem that is interesting to you.

19. Provided the development co-ordinator has a medium at least as good as the Internet, and knows how to lead without coercion, many heads are inevitably better than one.

Brooks' Law

Can any organization use the open source development model? The answer is (as we will see in Chapter 5, "Network Organizations") that it depends on the team leader. The most important issues in open source development are not technical—they are organizational. Organizational issues in an open source environment that builds upon voluntariness cannot be bought or forced—they must be earned.

The main business advantage is that open source can be a more effective way of developing software than the traditional way. This is somewhat contradictory. It is argued that programming time does not scale. In his classical book *The Mythical Man-Month* (Addison-Wesley, 1986), Frederick Brooks observed that adding manpower to a late software project makes it later. While working as a project manager of IBM OS/360 in the early 1960s, Brooks observed the diminishing output of multiple developers and that the man-month concept is a myth. The term *mythical man-month* is the concept of diminishing output of multiple developers even if all developers work on a given project from the very start. He observed that 1 programmer x 12 months does not equal 12 programmers x 1 month. The performance of programming teams does not scale in a linear fashion. Brooks found that when you throw additional programmers in a late project, you are only likely to make it later. The way to get a project back on schedule is to remove promised-but-not-yet-completed features, rather than adding programmers. He found that the complexity and communication costs of a project rise with the square of the number of developers, while the work produced only increases linearly. This claim has since become known as Brooks' Law. It is as true in 2000 as it was in 1975 when the book first published.

The mechanism behind Brooks' Law is that every new person in a team requires an administrative overhead that increases with the increasing number of team members. The communication between various team members increases as the number of meetings, project plans, performance reviews, management, and synchronizing of calendars and so on, grows. The increase grows exponentially as a combinatorial explosion such that the percentage of effort devoted to communication and administration becomes larger and larger.

But if Brooks' Law was the whole picture, Linux would be impossible. Open source uses the Internet to connect a geographically distributed pool of talents. Linux was the first project to make a conscious and successful effort to use the entire world as its talent pool. The global properties of the Internet potentially raise the quality of that pool in the absence of geographical barriers. Reducing the effects of distance does not eliminate other constraints under which such projects operate, but can dramatically increase the quality of the pool of developers.

While a cheap Internet was a necessary condition for the Linux model to evolve, it was not by itself a sufficient condition. Another vital factor was the development of a leadership style and set of cooperative customs that could allow developers to attract co-developers and get maximum leverage out of the medium. (See Chapter 5, "Network Organizations," for more information.)

Linus Torvalds argued that the person who understands and fixes the problem is not necessarily (or even usually) the person who first characterizes it:

> Somebody finds the problem and somebody else understands it. And I'll go on record as saying that finding it is the bigger challenge. But the point is that both things tend to happen quickly.

Linux guru Eric S. Raymond has identified this mechanism in "The Cathedral and the Bazaar" (O'Reilly & Associates, 1999, www.firstmonday.org/issues/issue3_3/raymond/index.html):

> Perhaps this should have been obvious (it's long been proverbial that "necessity is the mother of invention"), but too often software developers spend their days grinding away for pay at programs they neither need nor love. But not in the Linux world—which may explain why the average quality of software originated in the Linux community is so high.

To be fair, the average quality of software for the Windows community (low-cost commercial products, shareware, and freeware) is also exceptionally high despite weaknesses of the underlying operating system. Just look at a Windows games. Certainly Windows archives are "a great babbling bazaar of differing agendas and approaches" just like Linux archive sites.

Do Commercial Interests Combine with Voluntariness?

Will Mozilla succeed? Netscape's level of complexity, introduced by opening a preexisting project rather late in its development cycle, is probably the main reason for difficulties in attracting new developers. It is clear is that the complexity of Netscape's code represents a formidable barrier of entry that is not easily overcome by even highly motivated and qualified developers.

The pool of key developers is usually formed early in the life of a complex project when the project and program are still understandable and the intellectual and conceptual barrier to entry is low. After the project reaches a certain level of maturity, it essentially closes itself due to the "binarization" of code. The complexity of code makes the cost of entry into the project in mature stages much higher than at the beginning. It would be interesting to check this hypothesis for major programs like Perl, Apache, and Linux. Does the pool of developers for large projects remain more or less constant after the product reaches a certain level of maturity? If you are not onboard from the beginning, do you need to spend a lot of time and resources to catch up?

Certainly one striking example of the difficulty in dealing with large amounts of source code was the so-called Y2K problem. Ignoring all of the hype, the essence of the problem was that despite the availability of source code, many companies spent substantial amounts of time and money trying to fix one trivial logical error because some programs represent years with just two digits. The most important lesson here is that for old and complex software systems, even small problems are multiplied by the complexity and age of the underlying system and thus may turn into huge problems. Understanding legacy code without architectural blueprints is probably one of the most difficult activities for programmers. Often it is more difficult than writing new code. Therefore, in the absence of the original developers or substantial documentation, writing a completely new code instead of patching old code may be a viable and cost-effective strategy.

This and similar problems can be solved more efficiently working in an open source manner. It is a common wisdom that you can never prove that a program is faultless or that a text does not have any printer's errors. You can only prove that you find bugs. But four eyes see more than two.

This method of working is very similar to the statistical method called *Monte Carlo*. The Monte Carlo method provides approximate solutions to a variety of mathematical problems by performing statistical sampling experiments on a computer. The method applies to problems with no probabilistic content as well as to those with inherent probabilistic structure, much like the way bugs behave in a program.

Among all numerical methods that rely on N-point evaluations in M-dimensional space to produce an approximate solution, the Monte Carlo method has an absolute error of estimate that decreases as $N^{-1/2}$, whereas, in the absence of exploitable special structure all others have errors that decrease as $N^{-1/M}$ at best. In about 1970, the newly developing theory of computational complexity began to provide a more precise and persuasive rationale for employing the Monte Carlo method. The theory identified a class of problems for which the time to evaluate the exact solution to a problem within the class grows, at least, exponentially with M. Per Eric S. Raymond in "The Cathedral and the Bazaar" (O'Reilly & Associates, 1999, www.firstmonday .org/issues/issue3_3/raymond/index.html):

> In the bazaar view, on the other hand, you assume that bugs are generally shallow phenomena—or, at least, that they turn shallow pretty quick when exposed to a thousand eager co-developers pounding on every single new release. Accordingly you release often in order to get more corrections, and as a beneficial side effect you have less to lose if an occasional botch gets out the door.

Open Maintenance

Open source software is easy to maintain. "Given enough eyeballs, all bugs are shallow," is the law of Linus Torvalds. Only those who can access the source code are able to fix bugs themselves. As the source code can be inspected by anyone, errors are generally not only detected quickly, but also fixed on the spot. And because any programmer can contribute to the software, open source applications are sophisticated in an evolutionary process. In this case, the publicity about an interesting bug makes fixing it a worthwhile investment in the status game, as is often the situation with security bugs. As noted by Frederick Brooks in *The Mythical Man-Month* (Addison-Wesley, 1986):

> "The total cost of maintaining a widely used program is typically 40 percent or more of the cost of developing it. Surprisingly this cost is strongly affected by the number of users. More users find more bugs."

It's an old truth. More users find more bugs because adding more users adds more ways of stressing the program. Adding more beta-testers increases the probability of finding a specific bug. Every person has his or her own way of using the system, and therefore more potential bugs are discovered. In the specific context of debugging, this also tends to reduce duplication of effort.

Linux kernel versions are numbered in such a way that potential users can make a choice either to run the last version designated stable or to ride the cutting edge and risk bugs in order to get new features.

The problem is finding the complex bugs. Debugging a complex system is much more difficult than simply getting a huge number of eager programmers to analyze lines of code. For most complex projects, every second or third bug located and fixed increases the possibility of introducing another one. Linux distributions are a good illustration, as the latest versions in practice were beta versions, taking into account the number of bugs and fixes applied to them before they became designated as stable.

Certainly, if enough talented developers try to find the same bug it probably will be found sooner or later. But all bugs are not equal. There are three major types of bugs: code errors, logical errors, and architectural problems. The ordinary coding bugs are easy to find. The logical errors are somewhat harder to find and fix. The most complex bugs are consequences of architectural flaws such as security and limitations of tools used (mostly memory leaks and overflow).

Linux is known to have architectural problems, similar to any prototype system that is converted into a production system. The possibility of completely debugging Linux is related to making Linux architecturally superior to alternatives. There are pieces in the source that are good and pieces that are not. Many random developers have contributed to this source, and quality varies drastically. Some parts of the Linux source are ugly, and additional bugs could be easily introduced by fixing an existing one. Rewriting, not fixing, is more viable in these cases. Successful open source development should limit those who can directly contribute to the kernel to a few qualified developers on the core team. The open source model should be avoided in kernel development as much as possible. In Apache development, this is accomplished with the *meritocracy model*—the best programmers have the most influence over the code. This limits the number of programmers in the mission-critical parts of the software.

Summary

Brooks' law says that the more people working on the same problem, the more likely you delay the solution. The performance of programming teams does not scale linearly.

This is not the whole picture. Every new person in a team does require an administrative overhead that increases with the growing number of team members, but the global properties of the Internet potentially raise the quality of that pool in the absence of geographical barriers. Reducing the effects of distance does not eliminate other constraints under which such projects operate, but can dramatically increase the quality of the pool of developers. Linux was surely a successful project that used the entire world as its programming team.

But a vital factor was also the political attitude—the development of a new leadership style. An important aspect of open source is that the software is free. You are allowed to modify the source code without restrictions. It is possible to customize a program and pass on the modified program under the same conditions that applied to the original version.

The free exchange of information has been firmly embedded within the technologies and social protocols of the Internet. The idea of free software is also political and has its roots in libertarian opinion supported by anarchistic defenders.

The idea of open source is to take the concept of free software and make it a little more politically acceptable.

CHAPTER 3

The Open Source Philosophy

Free software is a matter of liberty, not price.
To understand the concept, you should think of free speech, not free beer.

**EXCERPT FROM *WHAT IS FREE SOFTWARE?*,
RICHARD M. STALLMAN, FREE SOFTWARE FOUNDATION, 1996
(WWW.GNU.ORG/PHILOSOPHY/FREE-SW.HTML)**

The concepts *open source* and *free software* are often confused. Both movements have a business perspective, but the starting points and the goals are very different.

The free software movement is a political movement with its roots in libertarian opinion supported by anarchistic defenders, conducted mainly by the Free Software Foundation and partly by the Electronic Frontier Foundation. The idea of open source software is to take the concept of free software and make it a little more politically acceptable. The goals of open source are just as broad as those of free software, but the measures are less extreme. Open source recognizes the idea that people wish to make money from their programs and tries to create a common ground between free and commercial software. The majority of the Linux community, however, find the open source system attractive for technical and commercial reasons, and don't care about freedom.

The free software movement and the open source movement are like two radical political parties within the same community. Although radical groups are known to fractionalize, organizations split because they disagree on details of strategy. They agree on the basic principles and disagree on practical recommendations. All too often they consider each other enemies and fight each other passionately.

The opposite is true regarding the free software movement and the open source movement. They disagree on the basic principles, but agree on most practical recommendations. The open source movement focuses on merely practical business goals, whereas the free software movement primarily is concerned about the kind of society we are going to live in.

The free software movement and the open source movement are not contradictory. They even work together on many specific projects such as the GNU/Linux operating system. But it is important to understand that open source and free software are not one and the same. The common enemy for both movements is proprietary software in general, but for various reasons. In the more radical groups, the enemy is Microsoft in particular. There is even a campaign to boycott Microsoft (www.vcnet.com/bms) and a lot of conspiracy theories about secret Microsoft protocols and formats floating around on the Internet.

Shareware, Freeware, and Public Domain

When talking about copyright and digital intellectual property, one should first consider the differences between shareware, freeware, and public domain.

Shareware and *freeware* apply to software circulating on the Internet that is free for anyone to distribute. Freeware is gratis, but shareware authors want to get paid.

The term freeware has no clear accepted definition, but it is commonly used for packages that permit redistribution but not modification. The source code is normally not available. These packages are not free software, as defined by the Free Software Foundation.

Shareware can be considered a *try and buy if you like* software. Shareware is software that comes with a permission to redistribute copies, but requires anyone who continues to use a copy to pay a license fee.

For most shareware, source code is not available, and thus you cannot modify the program. Shareware does not come with permission to make a copy and install it without paying a license fee. In practice, people often disregard the distribution terms and do this anyway, but nevertheless the terms don't permit it. Sometimes it is voluntary to pay—a popular way of both marketing and selling at the same time. Some of the most popular software on the market is shareware, like Winzip. Both shareware and freeware are copyrighted.

In the United States, it is possible to release one's hold of the ownership and transfer ownership to the *public domain*—public property or public information. Public domain is a U.S. legal concept that does not have any equivalent in Europe or Asia. In Europe, the best legislation corresponding to public domain is software or information where the copyright protection is no longer valid (works from owners that have been dead longer than 75 years). In Europe all information, whether it may be public domain, shareware or freeware, is copyright protected by common European law, even if the originator is from another country where he or she may have disclaimed the ownership. Such disclaimers are of no legal value in Europe. In other words, it is technically illegal to copy and duplicate any software whatsoever in Europe. Theoretically, a software developer could introduce a program as public domain in the United States, distribute it via the Internet, and be prosecuted in Sweden. On the other hand, no one will be prosecuted if the originator does not claim redress.

The borderline between what is considered public and what is private is fluid. Information of public interest, such as criminal records, could be insulting to a private person.

If software is public domain, the creator has transferred ownership to the public, but that does not imply that the person that has created the information or software is discharged from liability. Information or software that does not belong to anyone is considered public; that is, anyone has the right to use it and own it, but this is not the same thing as saying that no one has the right to own it. If no one claims the ownership, no one can take responsibility for the work. If cows are fed on common land, the grass will be consumed, and the cows will be without food. A public-domain system must have someone to take responsibility for the common goods; otherwise, the system doesn't last long. Any system without a responsible and final authority decays. Therefore, works without ownership do not exist, according to international laws. Without that regulation, virus programmers wouldn't be held responsible. Accordingly, ownership does not only involve the right to exclude others, but also the responsibility of maintenance of the property.

Ownership can be limited (a condominium that is shared between several people, for example). Oil or mineral deposits can be divided. Even the right to common air territory can be sold and conveyed. This also applies to public software. If software is free when it leaves the hands of its author, this does not necessarily mean it will be free software for everyone who has a copy of it. For example, public-domain software is free software, but anyone can make a proprietary modified version of it.

Likewise, many free programs are copyrighted, but distributed under a simple permissive license, which allows proprietary modified versions. One example of this is the X Window System. It was developed and released as free software with a permissive license from Massachusetts Institute of Technology. Soon, various computer companies adopted and added the software to their proprietary Unix systems in binary form only, and covered it with a nondisclosure agreement.

The developers of the X Window System did not consider this a problem. They even expected and intended this to happen. They only wanted the software to become a popular standard. Their goal was success, defined as having many users. They did not care whether these users had freedom, only that they should be numerous.

There are several ways to define free software. Freeware gives users and programmers freedom. Free software can easily become proprietary software. Based on the distribution terms of the MIT release, X Windows was free software. But bundled with the commercial Unix systems, it became proprietary software.

Defining public information is an old problem. During the nineteenth century, the U.S. government developed national farming by expressly prohibiting copyright on all government-owned information on agriculture. Agriculture schools were founded, manuals on modern farming were distributed free of charge, and there were grants for agricultural magazines. The goal was to make all information equally available to all farmers. The system was so successful that United States farming quickly became the most efficient in the world.

Open source is a way of giving back information to the public. A free market is based on competition. The strong competitor emerges, as the weaker one falls behind. In this environment, monopolies or oligopolies, which are considered contrary to general interest, can form. Problems with monopolies of software (e.g., Microsoft versus Netscape; Java versus Active X) is an example of this side effect of a free market.

The market is not concerned, however, with social redistribution. Important social issues such as basic education, basic health, or maintaining social—or even international—peace are left to the political sphere.

Therefore, more politically-oriented open source advocates argue that the evolution of intellectual property should not be treated only from judical or commercial viewpoints, but also from an ethical, philosophical, and ultimately, fundamental political slant. It is necessary to understand the lobbies at work and their motivations, and to determine from an enlightened vision, for the global good, the ethical assumptions that should guide the evolution of the law.

Electronic Frontier Foundation

The Electronic Frontier Foundation was founded in 1990 to create an opposite pole to the big commercial computer corporations. It is a nonprofit organization dedicated to preserving the rights of *digital citizens* working to protect the American Bill of Rights in all media.

The Electronic Frontier Foundation is of the opinion that big business has been alone in controlling ethics and laws, especially on the Internet. The Electronic Frontier Foundation believes that companies, by lobbying and using government authorities, are trying to create legal precedents that are completely contrary to the U.S. Constitution. While the Electronic Frontier Foundation regards the free flow of information as positive, it realizes that serious problems can arise, such as how to protect intellectual property rights. (The Electronic Frontier Foundation is also interested in how to determine which country's laws have jurisdiction over a global medium, how best to protect privacy, and how to protect children from information outrage.)

The founding principle of intellectual property laws is to protect general interest in ensuring universal dissemination of knowledge, creations, and inventions, while guaranteeing authors a protection of their rights for a limited period of time, after which their intellectual property falls into the public domain. The goal is to benefit humankind in the long-term by giving everyone access to knowledge and invention. During the French revolution, Le Chapelier established the principle of freedom of copy to encourage the freedom of commerce and industry and to avoid the bottlenecks, monopolies, and inefficiencies of an exclusive right to intellectual property. The general idea was to avoid the feudal privileges exclusively obtained from royalty until the Revolution. In the United States, at about the same time, Thomas Jefferson, promoter of the first public libraries, wrote in the *Writings of Thomas Jefferson*:

> He who receives an idea from me, receives instruction himself without lessening mine; as he who lights his taper at mine, receives light without darkening me. That ideas should freely spread from one to another over the globe, for the moral and mutual instruction of man, and improvement of his condition, seems to have been peculiarly and benevolently designed by nature, when she made them, like fire, expansible over all space, without lessening their density at any point, and like the air in which we breathe, move, and have our physical being, incapable of confinement or exclusive appropriation. Inventions then cannot, in nature, be a subject of property.

He was clearly in favor of "fair use" in matters of intellectual property, supporting general interest rather than just the protection of vested interests.

The concept of "commons" has existed since feudal times, and even earlier was conceptualized under the political category of *res publica*. In our globalized era, the Electronic Frontier Foundation considers it vitally and strategically important to recognize, promote, and strengthen the global public domain, be it physical, such as the Internet, or cultural and informational, such as masterpieces of the past or information produced on public funds.

While well-established legal principles and cultural norms give structure and coherence to uses of conventional media, the new digital media do not fit so easily into existing frameworks. The Electronic Frontier Foundation is dedicated to finding ways to resolve these and other conflicts, while ensuring that essential civil liberties are protected.

The Electronic Frontier Foundation wants to make the Internet truly useful and beneficial not just to a technical wealthy elite, but to everyone. This is achieved by keeping a free and open flow of information and communication.

This view has implications for open source software. An Internet governed by solely commercial forces cannot be truly open. Likewise political censorship prevents openness. Freedom in the sense of democracy and manifoldness benefits the collaborative way of working open source style. Both forces, especially the commercial, are strong against the political bearing of open source. This reaction is evident from the big international media companies on open sharing tools like Napster and Gnutella, which is a vital part of the open source culture. The traditional power elite—corporate executives, politicians, and heads of organizations—is losing influence in the incipient network society. More anonymous forces are taking power. It is easy to name the people who are losing power, but not quite so easy to identify who is gaining power. Open source and networking are fundamentally about interplay, processes no single actor controls. In a network, no individual can be held accountable. On the other hand, power is more evenly distributed in a network than in a hierarchy. The truly virtual enterprise is a company without a hierarchy. In that sense, open source and networking may imply a more democratic system than our traditional hierarchical society. The open source style of work is characterized by the globalization of various core functions and organizational flexibility at the expense of the traditional employed workforce. This makes historically unique productivity opportunities available. This new economy would be unthinkable without information technology.

The Electronic Frontier Foundation encourages and supports the development of new tools that will endow nontechnical users with full and easy access to computer-based telecommunications. The Electronic Frontier Foundation also supports an Open Platform model of the global information infrastructure, providing nondiscriminatory access, based on open, private-sector standards, and free from burdensome regulations and monopolization.

Among the founders are representatives from the industry such as Mitch Kapore, ex CEO in IBM's software company Lotus, leading IT journalists such as Ester Dyson, and politicians. John Perry Barlow is a retired cattle rancher, a lyricist for the Grateful Dead, and cofounder and executive chair of the Electronic Frontier Foundation. He describes himself as a cognitive dissident. In keeping with the mission of the organization, he is concerned about laws that restrict free speech on the Internet.

In *The Economy of Ideas, a Framework for Rethinking Patents and Copyright in the Digital Age,* John Perry Barlow (*Wired 2.03,* March 1994) argues that information should be free of charge, and that it is wrong to charge for information or software:

> Intellectual property law cannot be patched, retrofitted, or expanded to contain digitized expression any more than real estate law might be revised to cover the allocation of broadcasting spectrum (which, in fact, rather resembles what is being attempted here). We will need to develop an entirely new set of methods as befits this entirely new set of circumstances.

> Most of the people who actually create soft property—the programmers, hackers, and Net surfers—already know this. Unfortunately, neither the companies they work for nor the lawyers these companies hire have enough direct experience with nonmaterial goods to understand why they are so problematic. They are proceeding as though the old laws can somehow be made to work, either by grotesque expansion or by force. They are wrong...

> Throughout the history of copyrights and patents, the proprietary assertions of thinkers have been focused not on their ideas but on the expression of those ideas. The ideas themselves, as well as facts about the phenomena of the world, were considered to be the collective property of humanity. One could claim franchise, in the case of copyright, on the precise turn of phrase used to convey a particular idea or the order in which facts were presented.

> The point at which this franchise was imposed was that moment when the "word became flesh" by departing the mind of its originator and entering some physical object, whether book or widget. The subsequent arrival of other commercial media besides books didn't alter the legal importance of this moment. Law protected expression and, with few (and recent) exceptions, to express was to make physical.

> Protecting physical expression had the force of convenience on its side. Copyright worked well because, Gutenberg notwithstanding, it was hard to make a book. Furthermore, books froze their contents into a condition which was as challenging to alter as it was to reproduce. Counterfeiting and distributing counterfeit volumes were obvious and visible activities—it was easy enough to catch somebody in the act of doing. Finally, unlike unbounded words or images, books had material surfaces to which one could attach copyright notices, publisher's marques, and price tags.

> Mental-to-physical conversion was even more central to patent. A patent, until recently, was either a description of the form into which materials were to be rendered in the service of some purpose, or a description of the process by which rendition occurred. In either case, the conceptual heart of patent was the material result. If no purposeful object could be rendered because of some material limitation, the patent

was rejected. Neither a Klein bottle nor a shovel made of silk could be patented. It had to be a thing, and the thing had to work.

Thus, the rights of invention and authorship adhered to activities in the physical world. One didn't get paid for ideas, but for the ability to deliver them into reality. For all practical purposes, the value was in the conveyance and not in the thought conveyed.

In other words, the bottle was protected, not the wine.

Now, as information enters cyberspace, the native home of Mind, these bottles are vanishing. With the advent of digitization, it is now possible to replace all previous information storage forms with one metabottle: complex and highly liquid patterns of ones and zeros.

Even the physical/digital bottles to which we've become accustomed—floppy disks, CD-ROMs, and other discrete, shrink-wrappable bit-packages—will disappear as all computers jack-in to the global Net. While the Internet may never include every CPU on the planet, it is more than doubling every year and can be expected to become the principal medium of information conveyance, and perhaps eventually, the only one.

Once that has happened, all the goods of the Information Age—all of the expressions once contained in books or film strips or newsletters—will exist either as pure thought or something very much like thought: voltage conditions darting around the Net at the speed of light, in conditions that one might behold in effect, as glowing pixels or transmitted sounds, but never touch or claim to "own" in the old sense of the word...

The laws regarding unlicensed reproduction of commercial software are clear and stern...and rarely observed. Software piracy laws are so practically unenforceable and breaking them has become so socially acceptable that only a thin minority appears compelled, either by fear or conscience, to obey them. When I give speeches on this subject, I always ask how many people in the audience can honestly claim to have no unauthorized software on their hard disks. I've never seen more than 10 percent of the hands go up.

Today, a programmer cannot patent his or her idea—only the implementation of the idea. A program is considered the implementation of an idea. Therefore, the source code and binary are protected by copyright.

Barlow's thesis is that you cannot patent ideas, which is widely accepted. But he argues that the implementation should also be considered a tool without physical form, as it could be seen as an idea.

In the same sense that you cannot charge all work with payroll tax and VAT so that the fees will exceed the revenues, the software produced cannot claim copyright in every single instance. In that case, the market would suffocate.

Free Software Movement

The Free Software Foundation is probably the best-known mouthpiece for free software. Their goal is political and quite radical. The organization develops the software development toolbox GNU free of charge with the intention to "liberate the users from the power of software companies."

When Richard M. Stallman, founder of Free Software Foundation, talks about free software he is actually talking about free speech in general and scientific liberty in particular. The basic opinion of the Free Software Foundation is that source code is fundamental to the development of computer science. Freely available source code is necessary for innovation to continue.

Programmers have long known that they could work together in physical and temporal separation from each other. The phenomenon has grown to the extent that it has its own academic/professional literature and acronym: CSCW (Computer Supported Collaborative Work).

The Free Software Foundation argues that "Copyright is not a natural right, but an artificial government-imposed monopoly that limits the users' natural right to copy." They claim that computer users should be free to modify programs to fit their needs, and free to share software, because helping other people is the basis of society. Any nondisclosure agreement or license is a promise from the user not to help his or her neighbor, and thus a cooperating community is forbidden. All copyright restrictions made by the owners of proprietary software are interpreted as "if you share with your neighbor, you are a pirate. If you want any changes, beg us to make them."

The Free Software Foundation argues that "the proprietary software social system—the system that says you are not allowed to share or change software—is antisocial, is unethical, and simply wrong."

The Free Software Foundation's definition of free software has nothing to do with price. It is about freedom. A program is free software if:

➢ You have the freedom to run the program, for any purpose.

➢ You have the freedom to modify the program to suit your needs. (To make this freedom effective in practice, you must have access to the source code, because making changes in a program without having the source code is exceedingly difficult.)

➢ You have the freedom to redistribute copies, either gratis or for a fee.

➢ You have the freedom to distribute modified versions of the program, so that the community can benefit from your improvements.

A program is free software if the license conforms to all of these specifications. Thus, it is free to redistribute copies, either with or without modifications, either gratis or charging a fee for distribution, to anyone anywhere.

It is also permitted to make modifications and use them privately in work without even mentioning that they exist. If any changes are published, it is not required to notify anyone in particular, in any particular way.

In order to make changes, and to publish improved versions, the source code of the program must be available. Therefore, accessibility of source code is a necessary condition for free software.

Since *free* refers to freedom and not to price, there is no contradiction between selling copies and free software. In fact, the freedom to sell copies is crucial: Collections of free software sold on CD-ROMs are important for the community, and selling them is an important way to raise funds for free software development. Therefore, a program that people are not free to include on these collections is not free software.

Free Software Foundation uses the distribution term *copyleft*, which means all rights reversed. Copyleft uses copyright law, but flips it over to serve the opposite of its usual purpose. Instead of a means of privatizing software, it becomes a means of keeping software free.

The central idea of copyleft is that it gives everyone permission to run the program, to copy the program, to modify the program, and to distribute modified versions, but not the permission to add restrictions of their own. You can do what you want with the program, as long as you don't inhibit others from doing the same, either by charging them for the software or by restricting them from further licensing. Thus, the crucial freedoms that define free software are guaranteed to everyone who has a copy; they become inalienable rights.

For an effective copyleft, modified versions must also be free. This ensures that work based on copyleft becomes available to the community if it is published. When programmers who have jobs as programmers volunteer to improve copylefted software, it is copyleft that prevents their employers from making proprietary versions of the program.

Simple public domain publication will not work because some people will try to abuse this for profit. As long as we live in a world where legal abstractions such as copyright are necessary, as responsible artists or scientists we need formal legal abstractions of copyleft to ensure our freedom and the freedom of others.

To copyleft a program, the Free Software Foundation copyrights it, then adds distribution terms, which are legal instruments that give everyone the rights to use, modify, and redistribute the program's code or any program derived from it—but only if the distribution terms are unchanged. Thus, the code and the freedoms become legally inseparable.

Open Source

Most hackers don't have a problem with capitalism. But they do have a problem with closed source resulting in bad engineering results.

Open source promotes software reliability and quality by supporting independent peer review and rapid evolution of source code.

The Open Source Initiative is an organization founded by Eric S. Raymond to promote open source software and development strategies.

The OSI does not have a position on whether ideas can be owned, whether patents are good or bad, or any of the related controversies. The organization believes the economic self-interest arguments for open source are strong enough.

Linux is an open source operating system, and to date the most dramatically successful open source platform. Linux is very popular in education, Internet service applications, software development shops, and increasingly in small businesses. Several successful companies market Linux and Linux applications.

Linux isn't the whole open source story, however. There are many other open source systems and applications available, such as Netscape's Navigator and Communicator client line of Web browsers; Apache Web server was put together as literally "a patchy" set of updates to older software by a band of volunteer programmers. These open source programs are emerging not just as inexpensive software, but as more robust and dynamic alternatives to commercial software.

The OSI is a marketing program for open source. It strikes a blow for free software on pragmatic rather than ideological grounds. The basic idea has not changed, unlike the attitude.

The OSI created a definition for open source software, which is very much in the spirit of copyleft, but not as orthodox. It allows greater licensing liberties, such as more mixing between proprietary and open source software, and allows the use and redistribution of open source software without compensation or even credit.

The intent of the Open Source Definition (OSD) is to create a tangible proposal that captures the essence of what the software development community wants open source to mean—criteria that ensure that software distributed under an open source license will be available for independent peer review and continuous evolutionary improvement and selection, reaching levels of reliability and power no closed product can attain.

For the evolutionary process to work, the OSI had to counter short-term incentives for people to stop contributing to the software gene pool. This means the license terms must prevent people from locking up software where very few people can see or modify it.

The Open Source Definition (Version 1.7)

Open source doesn't just mean access to the source code. The distribution terms of open source software must comply with the following criteria.

1. Free Redistribution

The license may not restrict any party from selling or giving away the software as a component of an aggregate software distribution containing programs from several different sources. The license may not require a royalty or other fee for such sale.

Constraining the license to require free redistribution eliminates the temptation to throw away many long-term gains in order to make a few short-term sales dollars. If this was not the case, there would be much pressure for cooperators to defect.

2. Source Code

The program must include source code and must allow distribution in source code as well as compiled form. Where some form of a product is not distributed with source code, there must be a well-publicized means of obtaining the source code for no more than a reasonable reproduction cost—preferably, downloading via the Internet without charge. The source code must be the preferred form in which a programmer would modify the program. Deliberately obfuscated source code is not allowed. Intermediate forms such as the output of a preprocessor or translator are not allowed.

Access to unobfuscated source code is required because programs can't evolve without modification. Since the purpose is to make evolution easy, modification must be made easy.

3. Derived Works

The license must allow modifications and derived works, and must allow them to be distributed under the same terms as the license of the original software.

The mere ability to read source isn't enough to support independent peer review and rapid evolutionary selection. For rapid evolution, people need to be able to experiment with and redistribute modifications.

4. Integrity of the Author's Source Code

The license may restrict source code from being distributed in modified form only if the license allows the distribution of patch files with the source code for the purpose of modifying the program at build time. The license must explicitly permit distribution of software built from modified source code. The license may require derived works to carry a different name or version number from the original software.

Encouraging improvement is a good thing, but users have a right to know who is responsible for the software they are using. Authors and maintainers have a reciprocal right to know what they're being asked to support and to protect their reputations.

Accordingly, an open source license must guarantee that the source be readily available, but may require that it be distributed as pristine base sources plus patches. In this way, unofficial changes can be made available but readily distinguished from the base source.

5. No Discrimination against Persons or Groups

> The license must not discriminate against any person or group of persons.

In order to get the maximum benefit from the process, the maximum diversity of persons and groups should be equally eligible to contribute to open sources. Therefore it is forbidden for any open source license to lock anybody out of the process.

Some countries, including the United States, have export restrictions for certain types of software. An OSD-conformant license may warn licensees of applicable restrictions and remind them that they are obliged to obey the law; however, it may not incorporate such restrictions itself.

6. No Discrimination against Fields of Endeavor

> The license must not restrict anyone from making use of the program in a specific field of endeavor. For example, it may not restrict the program from being used in a business, or from being used for genetic research.

The major intention of this clause is to prohibit license traps that prevent open source from being used commercially. Open source supporters want commercial users to join the community, not feel excluded from it.

7. Distribution of License

> The rights attached to the program must apply to all to whom the program is redistributed without the need for execution of an additional license by those parties.

This clause is intended to forbid closing up software by indirect means such as requiring a nondisclosure agreement.

8. License Must Not Be Specific to a Product

> The rights attached to the program must not depend on the program's being part of a particular software distribution. If the program is extracted from that distribution and used or distributed within the terms of the program's license, all parties to whom the program is redistributed should have the same rights as those that are granted in conjunction with the original software distribution.

This clause forecloses yet another class of license traps.

9. License Must Not Contaminate Other Software

> The license must not place restrictions on other software that is distributed along with the licensed software. For example, the license must not insist that all other programs distributed on the same medium must be open source software.

Distributors of open source software have the right to make their own choices about their own software.

Yes, the GNU General Public License is conformant with this requirement. GNU General Public Licensed libraries contaminate only software to which they will actively be linked at runtime, not software with which they are merely distributed.

OSI Certified Mark

The OSI publishes standards for open source licenses. It created a certification mark, *OSI Certified*, to be applied only to software that is distributed under an open source license that meets criteria set by the OSI as representatives of the open software community.

While there is agreement that the broad term *open source* means approximately what is captured in the open source definition, the term has, ironically, now become so popular that it has lost some of its precision. The OSI strongly encourages everyone who cares about open source software to use the term only to describe licenses that conform to the definition, or software distributed under such licenses. But since the term has passed into more general use, the organization also encourages people to refer to the OSI Certified mark, which has precision and legal force in identifying software distributed under licenses that are known to meet the OSD requirements.

To be OSI certified, the software must be distributed under a license that guarantees the right to read, redistribute, modify, and use the software freely.

The aim is to make this mark become a widely recognized and valued symbol, clearly indicating that this software does, in fact, have the properties that the community has associated with the descriptive term open source.

Transcopyright

Ted Nelson, who invented hypertext in his system Xanadu (see Chapter 1, "An Open Source Primer"), works at the Keio University in Fujisawa, Japan. He and his Japanese development team are concentrating on repairing the World Wide Web, a bit at a time with components from Xanadu. The current fundamental work is *transcopyright*, a way of handling copyrights in compilated works.

Ted Nelson argues that all information is owned by somebody, but no one can own all information. The various bits and pieces from different people contribute to the whole, compiled, final work. If you put information in public domain, you don't necessarily need to give away the information, but this is different from traditional copyright. A big problem is how to pay the various contributors. As a solution, Ted Nelson came up with the concept of micro payments in 1992.

Transcopyright is exactly the opposite of open source. Nelson's ideas are interesting, but are founded on the notion that you want to control the copyright in every detail. Transcopyright meticulously looks after all versions of a document and exactly what every person has contributed.

Transcopyright is an academic tool mainly for use in research activities. The reason for open source is not that the technology is imperfect, but because there are other points of view of how copyright should work.

A New Openness

The idea of open source can be applied to any kind of digital information, not just computer software. The approach even works for developing content. The most successful is Netscape's Open Directory initiative. Once dubbed NewHoo, this Yahoo-like directory is built by international volunteers, just as programmers around the globe built Apache.

Four years ago, five of the six top search engines on the Web were based on computers performing automated searches. Today, five of the top six search engines rely on humans to catalog and categorize the vast universe of Web pages. Amazingly, four of the five manually-produced search engines rely on the same army of unpaid volunteers, the Open Directory project (www.dmoz .org). If Linux and Apache rely on the technical skills of thousands of computer programmers, the Open Directory project relies on nothing more complicated than the curiosity of ordinary Web surfers. Today, more that 20,000 of them have signed up to keep track of current listings in categories from business to health to technology.

As with open source code, the directory is freely available to any Web site that wants it. As more sites use the directory, more volunteer editors will likely be drawn in.

The open source model may be replicated in many fields, as it's a natural consequence of the distributed nature of the Web.

With computers, perfect copies of a digital work can easily be made, modified, and distributed by others, with no loss to the original work. Individuals interact and share information, and then react and build upon it; this is not only natural, it is also the only way for individuals to succeed in a community. In essence, the idea of open source is basic to the natural propagation of digital information among humans in a society. This is why the traditional notion of copyright does not really make sense on the Internet.

Open source is not merely an exotic idea from a group of radicals. Secretary-General Kofi Annan and recently Dr. Gro Harlem Brundtland have emphasized the need for free and uncontrolled access to information and the importance of easy border-less knowledge spreading. At the Global Knowledge Conference in 1999, Secretary-General Kofi Annan noted:

> The great democratizing power of information has given us all the chance to effect change and alleviate poverty in ways we cannot even imagine today. With information on our side, with knowledge a potential for all, the path to poverty can be reversed.

> Knowledge is power. Information is liberating. Education is the premise of progress, in every society, in every family. We at the United Nations are convinced that information is a great democratizing power waiting to be harnessed to our global struggle for peace and development.

> We believe this because we are convinced that it is ignorance, not knowledge that makes enemies of men. It is ignorance, not knowledge that makes fighters of children. It is ignorance, not knowledge that leads some to advocate tyranny over democracy. It is ignorance, not knowledge that makes some think that human misery is inevitable. It is ignorance, not knowledge that makes others say that there are many worlds, when we know that there is one.

> Information and freedom are indivisible. The information revolution is unthinkable without democracy, and true democracy is unimaginable without freedom of information. This is information's new frontier, this is where the United Nations pledges its commitment, its resources and its strength.

Similarly, Dr. Gro Harlem Brundtland, Secretary-General of the WHO, said the following at the Healthy Planet Conference of June 18, 1999:

> We have learned that we cannot hope for change towards sustainable development without democracy, freedom of speech and access to information.
>
> More than a billion fellow human beings have been left behind in the health revolution. A lot more dedicated work is required for us to reach health for all. There is a need to be expanding the knowledge base that made the 20th century revolution in health possible.
>
> The challenge now is to make sure that the information which is produced reaches those who make the critical decisions.

The Arhus convention, advocated by the World Health Organization (WHO), states that "public participation and access to information are increasingly recognized as essential elements in making the much needed transition toward health-enhancing and sustainable forms of development; it further sets out essential elements for access to information held by public authorities, namely, a general presumption in favor of access."

Additionally, this request is all about Chapter 40 of Agenda 21 of the Rio declaration on sustainable development: (sharing) information for decision making, which was greatly supported by all U.N. agencies. The United Nations supports the idea of distribute assets, like information among other things. Therefore the United Nations have adopted open source as a mean for distributing information and knowledge.

Open Content

There is a fundamental difference between code and content. It's a problem many Internet users share: How do you allow successive modifications of online materials without losing the credibility of the original?

There are an infinite number of ways to code a program so that it fulfills a specific purpose. Even the subjective part of coding, such as decisions about specific implementation issues, can be compared objectively in terms of reductions in file size, memory footprint, or execution time. The improvement of a program can be measured, regardless of how it is produced.

David Wiley at Brigham Young University has modeled an Open Publication License (OPL) on the agreements that allow open source programmers to constantly and collectively improve free software. In fact, Richard M. Stallman and Eric S. Raymond helped him draft the license.

The OPL grants anybody permission to modify and redistribute the materials, provided changes are marked and the resulting work is also put out under the license. Wiley set up a repository for all OPL works at the OpenContent Web site (www.opencontent.org). The repository contains works ranging from experimental art to university course materials.

Such crossover from the free-content community to the for-profit realm are most valuable when ideas are new and changing fast, and where mindshare is more important than marketshare. This way, a work could benefit from online peer review and peer improvement while a hard-copy version's publisher would be protected from its competitors.

Open Journalism

A news article is a different matter. How do you compare one piece of prose with another? While there are some comparatively objective sides to prose, such as mechanics or accuracy of factual information, it is a much more subjective matter. Bad code is objectively bad. When someone inserts "not" into a sentence, however, there is often no quick, objective way to tell whether the content of the prose has been corrupted.

An open source project must always be coordinated by a "project maintainer," in Eric S. Raymond's words. In an open content project, it is an editor. An editor has the same responsibilities as the open source software project maintainer, but must be accountable for factual accuracy. For example, while one open source Civil War project might interpret the causes of the recent unpleasantness to be issues of states' sovereignty and another might explain it in terms of human rights, we would expect both projects to be as factually accurate as possible, and hold the project maintainer accountable to see that they are. The critical issue for the editor is criticism of the sources.

As a journalist, I know that professional journalism is a culture with a strong sense of the value of certain kinds of information. The ability to sort information into what's newsworthy and what's not is probably the guiding principle of the entire profession of journalism. The strongest praise people in a newsroom can say about their colleagues is that "they have a nose for news." It's that ability to recognize instinctively what is news—and the corollary ability to ignore automatically anything that's not news—which separates journalists from outsiders.

Open source journalism is more than just a modest play on words. Professional journalism is addicted to anonymous sources, sources that always have a hidden agenda known to reporters, but never explained to readers or viewers.

Bart Preecs is a market analyst and journalist who has started "Open Source Journalism: An Alternate Strategy For Using The Internet To Empower Citizens And Strengthen Democracy" (www.makeyourownmedia.org). He believes that open source journalism could do to our centralized media cathedrals (like the *Wall Street Journal*, the *New York Times*, CBS, or PBS) what Linux programmers are doing to Microsoft. The free software movement keeps Microsoft executives awake at nights because the people creating Linux or Apache are not doing it for the money or the stock options. They're creating computer code that competes with Windows 2000 for love.

In the same way, we could create an alternative to advertiser-filtered, controversy-driven, celebrity-obsessed, insider-based professional journalism. Open source journalism would be amateur journalism; journalism produced by citizens, scholars, community activists, and others for love of the idea of creating, organizing, or deploying the information that could save our planet and our souls.

Although many news organizations have invested millions of dollars in Web-based delivery systems, those systems often deliver nothing more than re-purposed content from existing publications.

For a better model of how to use the Web as a publishing resource, we should stop thinking about daily newspapers as the model. Given that the primary characteristic of the Web is its ability to gather, organize, and retrieve large volumes of information, it's a better model than the daily newspaper, which even in its most developed form is a hastily gathered collection of random summaries of disconnected events.

Bart Preecs argues that a better model is an almanac. This may be counter-intuitive, but the advantages should be clear. Where newspapers are random collections, almanacs are systematic and organized. Where news organizations focus almost exclusively on the latest developments, almanacs focus on long-term trends. Publishing an almanac in weekly cycles may produce more useful journalism than trying to supplement daily newspaper cycles with hourly updates.

An effort to create an alternative model of news and longer-term information gathering and distributing could also build on the strong work being done by Redefining Progress and the Friends of the Earth Index of Sustainable Economic Welfare project. These groups question the validity of official statistics collected by economists, arguing that measures such as Gross National Product do not accurately measure either quality of real life or the long-term impact of the economy on the natural environment.

Open Law

Harvard Law School professor Lawrence Lessig is testing the idea that the "parallel processing" that goes on in open source software development can be used effectively, in some cases, in developing a legal argument.

Lessig's new model called Openlaw, is an experiment in crafting legal argument in an open forum. With public assistance, he will develop arguments, draft pleadings, and edit briefs in public, online. Nonlawyers and lawyers alike are invited to join the process by adding thoughts to the "brainstorm" outlines, drafting and commenting on drafts in progress, and suggesting reference sources.

Building on the model of open source software, Openlaw works from the hypothesis that an open development process best fits the distributed resources of the Internet community. By using the Internet the public interest can speak as loudly as the interests of corporations. Openlaw is therefore a large project built through the coordinated effort of many small and moderate contributions.

Lessig is testing the approach with Eldred v. Reno, a challenge to the U.S. Sonny Bono Copyright Term Extension Act. Passed in October 2000, the law extends to 70 years the copyright protection that for most works used to be valid until 50 years after the author's death. In January, Eric Eldred, founder of Eldritch Press, a company that publishes the full text of rare and out-of-print books on its Web site, challenged the law in a federal lawsuit. Now Eldred has some volunteer help from teams of law students at Harvard and at the Intellectual Property Clinic at the University of California at Berkeley's Boalt Hall School of Law. The Berkman Center for Internet and Society has published the students' potential legal arguments on the Openlaw site (www.openlaw.org). Site visitors are invited to brainstorm and send in comments, suggestions, and recommended reference sources to help shape the development of the case.

Lawrence Lessig is a U.S. leading scholar on the challenges of legislating cyberspace. He was recently summoned by U.S. District Judge Thomas Penfield Jackson to testify as a special master in the Microsoft antitrust trial. He believes the broad issue is preserving the Internet as an intellectual space for comment and publication. That space is being threatened by the increasing legal trend of *propertization*.

Public access to literature, art, music, and film is essential to preserving and building upon cultural heritage. Many of the most important works of American culture have drawn upon the creative potential of the public domain. Frank Capra's "It's a Wonderful Life" is a classic example of a film that did not enjoy popular success until it entered the public domain. Other icons such as Snow White, Pinocchio, Santa Claus, and Uncle Sam grew out of public domain figures.

The Berkman Center for Internet and Society has introduced the term *counter-copyright*. As an alternative to the exclusivity of copyright, counter-copyright invites others to use and build upon a creative work. By encouraging the widespread dissemination of such works, the counter-copyright campaign fosters a rich public domain.

The idea surrounding the counter-copyright campaign is fairly easy to understand. If you place the counter-copyright [cc] icon at the end of your work, you signal to others that you are allowing them to use, modify, edit, adapt, and redistribute the work that you created. The counter-copyright is not a replacement for an actual copyright, rather it is a signal that you as the creator are willing to share your work. The counter-copyright strips away the exclusivity that a copyright provides and allows others to use your work as a source or a foundation for their own creative ideas. The counter-copyright initiative is analogous to the idea of open source in the software context.

Summary

Open source is a general concept and not unique to software development, even if it was first adapted in the programming community. There are experiments with open source in several other areas like journalism and law. Open source in a broader sense has both economical and political consequences.

Open source is a vital part of the *new economy*, but it is important not to confuse free software with open source. It is also important to know the differences in jurisdiction. Free software in the public domain—public property or public information—is a U.S. legal concept. In Europe all information, whether it may be public domain, shareware, or freeware, is copyright protected by common European law, even if the originator is from another country where he or she may have disclaimed the ownership.

Controlling intellectual property is the basis for almost all modern businesses, and open source changes this entirely.

CHAPTER 4

Open Source and the Internet Economy

In ecology, as in economics, TANSTAAFL (There Ain't No Such Thing As A Free Lunch) is intended to warn that every gain is won at some cost. Failure to recognize the "no free lunch" law causes the buffalo-hunter mentality syndrome—the unthinking assumption that there will always be plenty because there always has been plenty.

DR. ROBERT W. PREHODA, SCIENCE FICTION WRITER,
MALTHUSIAN CRISIS AND METHUSELAH'S CHILDREN,
ACE, 1980

From the Oxford English Dictionary to rap music, open source development has always been with us to some degree. Since the middle of the nineteenth century, contributors to the Oxford English Dictionary have defined words and sent them to a centralized location to be gathered, criticized, sorted, and published.

The music business has always made a living on borrowing. As long as you stay within certain copyright laws, you can take chunks of other people's compositions and work them into your own. Sampling, DJ-ing, and mixing are already blurring property rights within modern dance music. But sampling is not a new phenomenon. All of the classical masters borrowed as well. Old Renaissance music was produced with a manual form of musical sampling; the composers borrowed ruthlessly from each other. Great composers have always incorporated folk music into their own work, like Georges Bizet's "Carmen" and "L'Arlesienne," "The Shaker Song" in Aaron Copland's "Appalachian

Spring," and "Moldau" by Bedrich Smetana, where the Swedish folk song "Ack Värmeland du sköna" is the main theme, well known to all young school children in Sweden.

Musicians are now using the Internet for the digital distribution of their recordings, through distribution channels like Napster and Gnutella, and by Web sites like MP3. By giving away their own work to this network community, individuals get fame and the community gets free access to a larger amount of music in return. And by using a shareware-type of economy, in combination with almost no distribution cost, individual musicians can earn a living from it.

It all depends on how you price information. Information is costly to produce, but very cheap to reproduce. Once the first copy has been produced, most costs are sunk and cannot be recovered. *Sunk costs* are costs that are not recoverable if production is halted. If you invest in a new computer and you decide that you don't need it, you can reclaim a part of the cost by selling the equipment. If your production effort (such as the creation of software, a book, a film, a music CD, etc.) flops, however, there isn't much of a resale market for it. Sunk costs generally have to be paid up front, before the production begins, as well as marketing and promotion costs.

But if the product succeeds, multiple copies can be produced at roughly constant per-unit costs. The cost of an extra digital copy is negligible. There are no natural capacity limits for additional copies.

Following this reasoning, you don't lose any money if you don't get paid for a copy—you merely miss an opportunity for additional revenue. If there were extremely high penalties for stealing the information, it is likely that the person who didn't pay wouldn't have paid in the first place. Instead, he or she would have chosen to ignore the information and made revenue a moot point.

Open as a Business Strategy

Openness arises naturally when multiple products must work together, making coordination in product design essential. Openness may be in the eye of the beholder. The term *open* means many things. The Unix X/Open consortium defines *open systems* as:

> Systems and software environments based on standards which are vendor independent and commonly available.

Many IT companies claim to be open systems. Even Microsoft claims Windows is an open system, as the application programming interfaces (APIs) are public. Two kinds of open business strategies are:

➤ A strategy in which anyone has the right to make products complying with a standard.

➤ An alliance in which each member is allowed to make products complying with a standard.

The membership approach has been popular in the IT industry (Open Software Foundation and X/Open, for example). The success has been limited due to lack of a clear sponsor, internal disagreement about directions, lack of a clear target, and because the standard groups were formed mainly as marketing gimmicks.

Open Is Not Always What It Seems to Be

Open standards often give rise to multiple, incompatible versions. The classic example is Unix. During the 1980s several different hardware vendors including IBM, Hewlett-Packard, Sgi, and Novell, created their own flavors. Sun started cleverly by claiming their Unix operating system to be a "standard." There were several efforts to agree on a Unix standard, but all these failed due to infighting among hardware and software vendors.

Serious efforts were not made until Windows NT had taken a severe market share of the operating systems market. In March 1993, Novell tried to take leadership by buying Unix System Labs from AT&T. Novell gave the trademark "Unix" to the X/Open consortium based in London.

X/Open was founded in 1985 by 14 IT companies to promote standardization work around Unix. The idea was to let any company call its product Unix as long as it met the X/Open specifications. Novell tried to get positive feedback from high expectations by setting a standard. Novell continued marketing its own flavor of Unix, UnixWare, hoping to give Unix new momentum and attempting to get UnixWare a decent share of the growing Unix market. The plan failed. IBM, Hewlett-Packard, Sun, and SCO expressed concerns that Novell was attempting to make UnixWare the de facto standard. Meanwhile, Windows NT continued to make headway in the traditional Unix markets.

Nowadays full openness is considered the only credible approach. However, it is not restricted to a formal standards setting. It is a way of overcoming a deadlock in which no single company is in a position to force its preferred standard without widespread support.

One way to achieve openness is to do as Novell did, that is, to place the technology in the hands of a neutral party. But as we can see from the Novell lesson, this move can be questioned. Do the parties really want full openness when the user base grows or competition shifts? Usually newcomers want openness to neutralize established technology. Dominant and established players resist openness.

In their book *Information Rules: A Strategic Guide to the Network Economy* (Harvard Business School Press, 1998), Carl Shapiro and Hal R. Varian identify four generic strategies in network markets, as shown in Table 4.1.

There are two strategies for creating a successful new technology in the market: The *evolution strategy* of compatibility and the *revolution strategy* of compelling performance. These strategies reflect an underlying tension when forces of innovation combine with network effects. Is it better to come up with the best product possible and make all old technology obsolete (the revolutionary approach) or to give up some performance to ensure compatibility and thus ease consumer adoption (the evolutionary approach)?

Either of these approaches can be combined with openness or control. The left-hand column in Table 4.1 represents the decision to retain proprietary control. The right-hand column represents the decision to open up the technology to others. The strategies that emerge are:

➢ Controlled migration

➢ Open migration

➢ Performance play

➢ Discontinuity

Controlled migration **is where consumers are offered a new and improved technology that is compatible with their existing technology.** But the technology is proprietary. Upgrades and updates fit into this category. This is the strategy usually chosen by companies that dominate their market, like Microsoft and Intel.

Open migration **is very friendly to consumers.** A new product is supplied by many vendors and requires little switching costs. Modems and fax machines fit into this category. Each new generation conforms to an open standard. Companies that have manufacturing skills and scale of economics have adopted this strategy, such as Japanese electronic companies.

Performance play **involves the introduction of a new, incompatible technology over which the vendors keep strong control (a new product category, for example).** This applies to all new inventions. Innovation companies adopt this strategy.

Table 4.1   Generic Network Strategies

	CONTROL	**OPENNESS**
Compatibility (Evolution)	Controlled migration	Open migration
Performance (Revolution)	Performance play	Discontinuity

Discontinuity **refers to the situation in which a new product or technology is incompatible with existing technology, but is available from multiple suppliers.** The introduction of the CD and the 3.25 inch floppy disk are examples of discontinuity. Companies that have manufacturing skills and scale of economics have adopted this strategy.

Try It First Information

An *experience good* is something consumers must experience to value. Virtually any new product on the market is made an experience good, and marketers have developed strategies such as free samples, promotional pricing, and testimonials to help consumers learn about new goods.

Information is an experience good every time it's consumed. How do you know whether the new album with the newly discovered Beatles recordings is worth the money until you've heard it? You don't. Information businesses like music, magazine, and movie industries have various strategies to get cautious consumers to overcome their reluctance to buy information. You can read the headlines at the newsstand, you can listen to top lists on the radio, and watch previews at the movies. But that is not enough. Branding and reputation are an essential part as well. The main reason that we buy Beatles music today is that it's a safe bet. It stands for authority, a quality brand identity, and fan club loyalty. The Beatles "brand" conveys a message to potential listeners about the quality of the content, thereby overcoming the experience good problem endemic to information goods.

The greatest threat to the commercial music corporations comes from the flexibility and spontaneity of the gift economy. The legal hullabaloo around Napster does not lessen the high marketing value the technology gives musicians who use the medium for their own purpose. Not surprisingly, the media business is worried about the increased opportunities for the piracy of copyrighted recordings over the Net. After it is completed, a new track can quickly be made freely available to a global audience. If someone likes the tune, they can download it for personal listening, use it as a sample, or make their own remix. Out of the free circulation of information, musicians can form friendships, work together, and inspire each other.

I believe that content owners tend to be too conservative with respect to the management of their intellectual property. The introduction of cheap production and distribution mechanisms is not new, nor are means to control it. In the Middle Ages, professors used to lecture in darkened rooms so that the students couldn't take notes.

Libraries first appeared to threaten the printing industry, but ended up expanding it. "Low-brow" and "vulgar" novels rather than edifying religious tracts appealed to large diverse groups of readers. The libraries in the eighteenth century consisted mostly of English novels. The availability of inexpensive entertainment motivated many to learn to read.

Printers found that people didn't really care about expensive high-quality books. Printers who understood this changed their business model. They began using new printing technology from linotype and monotype to produce high volumes of cheap pulp magazines and tabloids to satisfy the new literate class of people for whom books were information and not an investment. Also, as the mass market grew, people started to buy rather than rent books. At that time libraries had a rental fee just like today's video rental stores.

Thus it was the presence of the libraries that killed the old publishing model of expensive books for the wealthy, but a new business model of mass-market books killed old libraries that charged for lending.

New technology creates opportunities for new business models, but new business models also create a demand for new technology. New business models have new problems that have to be solved. The Internet made the business model of open source possible, which threatens the old copyright industry—software, information, and media industries. The music industry sees the Internet as one giant out-of-control copying machine. But the Internet also allows for new and interesting technologies that utilize the open source business model. It is a fantastic new medium for distribution and collaboration.

Technically, every document on the Internet involves copying material from one computer to another. The architecture of the system assumes that multiple copies of documents can easily be cached around the network. As Tim Berners-Lee (the inventor of the World Wide Web) points out in his essay *The World Wide Web: Past, Present and Future* (IEEE Computer, Volume 29, Number 11, November 1996, page 69–77):

> Concepts of intellectual property, central to our culture, are not expressed in a way which maps onto the abstract information space. In an information space, we can consider the authorship of materials, and their perception; but ... there is a need for the underlying infrastructure to be able to make copies simply for reasons of [technical] efficiency and reliability. The concept of 'copyright' as expressed in terms of copies made makes little sense.

Berners-Lee asserts that the design of the World Wide Web makes intellectual property technically and socially obsolete.

The media and software industries fear the that advances in digital reproduction are making piracy of copyright material easier, which is true. For the owners of intellectual property, the Internet can only make the situation worse. In contrast, the academic gift economy welcomes technologies that improve the availability of data. Users should always be able to obtain and manipulate information with minimum impediments.

But it's not a matter of the death of the copyright law. These principles are old and tried, and have outlived many hundred of years of technology changes. The basic principles of intellectual property rights are still valid (though questioned, but that is not a new issue either). Every new reproduction technology, from the printing press to the Internet, has brought forth predictions that it would destroy the industry. That has never happened, only the old business models were broken. The copyright industry is now depicting the Internet as a threat to Western society, but Hollywood was also frightened by the advent of videotape recorders. The TV industry filed suits to prevent home copying of TV programs. All of these attempts failed when the video rental stores appeared and brought films to the masses by renting both the video machine and the movie. Disney attempted to distinguish video sales and rentals through licensing arrangements, but the owners of these stores wouldn't cooperate. Ironically, Hollywood now makes more money from video sales than from cinema shows for most productions. The availability of inexpensive content made people watch more film, as the availability of inexpensive books made people read more.

There are a lot of new models waiting to be discovered and implemented. The new opportunities offered by free information far outweigh the problems. It's all a matter of perception. Either you look for problems or you look for new opportunities.

Standards

For many technologies, consumers benefit from using a standard format or standard system. But not all standards are alike. A critical distinguishing feature is the magnitude of switching costs, or more generally the adoption costs, for each rival technology. *Adoption cost* is the price consumers pay to adopt a new technology. *Switching cost* is the price consumers pay when they switch from an old technology to a new one (e.g., LPs to CDs; VHS to DVD). If the technologies are incompatible with each other, the switching costs are high. If they are compatible, the switching costs are low.

In their book, *Information Rules: A Strategic Guide to the Network Economy* (Harvard Business School Press, 1998), Carl Shapiro and Hal R. Varian identified four types of standards wars, according to how compatible each player's proposed new technology is to the current technology (see Table 4.2).

The evolution versus revolution war is a contest between backward compatibility (evolution) and superior performance (revolution). An example of this

Table 4.2 Types of Standards Wars

	COMPATIBLE	INCOMPATIBLE
Compatible	Rival evolutions	Evolution versus revolution
Incompatible	Revolution versus evolution	Rival revolutions

concept is an upstart fighting against an established technology that is offering compatible upgrades, for example, Linux versus Microsoft.

If the new technologies are compatible with the old technology, but incompatible between themselves, the battle is one of rival evolutions. The battle of 56k modems is an example of such a fight as between US Robotics X2 and Rockwells K56flex. Both are compatible with older modems, but they cannot communicate with each other at full speed.

If the new technology offers backward compatibility and the older technologies don't, we have evolution versus revolution, and vice versa. The battle between Lotus 1-2-3 and Excel followed this pattern.

If neither technology is backward compatible, we have rival revolutions. The contest between Sony PlayStation and Nintendo 64 follows this pattern.

Network Effects

When the value of a product to one user depends on how many other users of the same product there are, economists say that this product exhibits *network effects*. This system delivers increased return as it expands. Communication technologies are a prime example.

This is a central feature of the Internet economy. According to Bob Metcalfe, the inventor of Ethernet, and later discussed by Kevin Kelly, editor of *Wired*, in his book *New Rules for the New Economy: Ten Radical Strategies for a Connected Word* (Viking Penguin, USA, 1998), the value of a network increases exponentially in relation to the number of nodes it contains:

> As the number of nodes in a network increases arithmetically, the value of the network increases exponentially.

The basic idea, known as Metcalfe's Law, is that as the number of people connected to a network increases, the greater the utility to all parts of the system. Every new participant adds value for all the old participants in the network. The effect is an explosion of dissemination and expansion, where new users benefit all participants. The value of becoming a participant, of "boarding the train," is constantly increasing as well.

Metcalfe's Law is more a rule than a law, but it does arise in a relatively natural way. If there are n people in a network, and the value of the network to each of them is proportional to the number of other users, then the total value of the network to all the users is proportional to $n * (n - 1) = n2 - n$. A tenfold increase in the size of the network leads to a hundredfold increase in its value.

The most frequently used example of this principle at work is the fax machine. The first fax machine had no value because it had nothing to communicate with. The next fax machine made the first one much more valuable. The third made the first two more valuable, and so on. Ultimately, the value of the "fax machine network" far exceeded the simple resale value of any individual machine. The same goes for telephones, email, Internet access, and modems.

Since no one actually owns the fax machine network, nor the Internet, the only revenue, aside from the cost of a phone call, comes from selling the machines themselves—a low-margin, high-volume activity commodity market. Likewise, email is ubiquitous, yet almost no one sells email programs. Most consumers receive email programs bundled with Windows or their Web browser.

Open source is a variant of the network effect. Operating systems like Linux and Windows form a *virtual* network. Each user benefits from a larger network, since this facilitates the exchange of files and tips. The systems enjoy a significant competitive advantage over less popular systems, which encourages programmers to develop software for the systems.

The key challenge for success is to obtain a critical mass. The market will build itself once you have a large enough customer base. A superior technology, however, is not enough. To penetrate the market you also need to set the right price.

Expectation Management

In competing to become a standard, or at least to achieve critical mass, consumer expectations are critical. The product that is expected to become the standard will become the standard. Self-fulfilling expectations are an important mechanism of positive-feedback economics.

Companies participating in markets with strong network effects seek to convince customers that their products will ultimately become the standard, so that a rival product will disappear.

IBM's and Microsoft's strategy of announcing their intentions is a good example of expectation management. Also, pre-announcements of coming products, so-called *vaporware*, raise the expectations. IBM invented the technique in the 1970s and was accused of using pre-announcements to stifle competition. In the middle of the 1980s, when Borland released the spreadsheet Quattro Pro, Microsoft was quick to counter with a press release describing how much better the next release of its spreadsheet program, Excel, would be. When network effects are strong, product announcements can be as important as the actual introduction of products.

Critical mass, customer expectations, and rapid technology development make the timing of strategic moves important. Internet companies often accuse old companies of moving too late. If you are late to market, you risk missing the market entirely, especially if customers become locked into rival technologies.

But moving too early can sometimes be even worse. Being first to market can backfire if superior technology will soon arrive. Being a pioneer means making compromises in technology, having no allies, taking all initial costs, and using untested business models. Many technologies and applications have suffered an early death this way.

IBM is seldom the first in a market—the company learns from the mistakes of early adopters and enters the market as a good second.

Positive Feedback

Technologies that have strong network effects tend to exhibit long lead times followed by explosive growth. The pattern results from *positive feedback*. As the installed base of users grows, more and more users find adoption worthwhile. Eventually, the product achieves critical mass and takes over the market.

The basic fax technology was patented in 1843, but faxes remained a niche product until the mid 1980s. During a five-year period, the demand for and supply of fax machines exploded. Before 1982, almost no one had a fax machine. After 1987, the majority of businesses had one or more.

The Internet follows the same pattern. The first email message was sent in 1969, but up until the mid-1980s email was used only by scientists. As of August 2000, 63 percent of Swedish citizens over 12 years of age have personal email addresses.

Someone must start the positive feedback, but once started it runs by itself. The more widespread the product, the more likely it is to be selected. In this way, a popular product can become the de facto market standard.

To create standards, producers of consumer products often cooperate and deliberately try to achieve positive feedback. This is what Larry Ellison, CEO of Oracle, calls *coopetition*. All actors both cooperate and compete to create a larger market.

But there is a big difference between the consumer product companies and the IT industry. The IT industry uses licenses to earn money. Licenses in the consumer market are only a way of paying the administrative costs in the standardization work. The consumer products industry earns money on products, not licenses. They treat standards and licenses as a way of creating markets no single actor can afford to create. The collective effort of many actors can create the volume needed to create a profitable market.

The best way to create a large user base is to give something for free. Giving something away for free offers benefits in other ways, like service, sponsoring, or even charity. The European GSM mobile phone market was created by two mechanisms. First, the telecom operators changed their billing to "caller pays all." The receiver of a mobile phone call does not pay anything. Second, they gave away the telephones more or less for free, but made a profit on the calls. Netscape grabbed the Web browser market by giving away its product. It compensated by selling the server software and customer support. Internet consumer portals are giving away information to try to capture an audience because of its content and selling that audience to online marketers. The presumption is that by giving away products, companies can build loyalty, and thereafter capture revenue for a premium product or ancillary service.

Anything essential in a network market can be used to create a user base: products, services, and even licenses. For example, Sony was once the leader in the VCR market with its Betamax system. The company charged a license fee. JVC quickly realized the value of the growing video rental stores and instead gave their VHS licenses for free to the movie industry to create content, and by doing that, create a user demand for video machines.

The network effect is of importance for open source. The faster a company can spread its product, the bigger the chances that the product will become a standard. If the company is sharing key technology or technology that facilitates the use of a product they own, it creates favorable conditions for the spreading of the product.

But on the Internet, scarcity of information begins to disintegrate. If everyone is giving away goods at or below cost to gather networks of people, then networks of people may themselves become commodities. Indeed, as such networks proliferate, the value of providing a new network diminishes, while the difficulty of attracting members' attention increases.

Investors in Internet companies that equate *user base* with *market capitalization* are like the old Roman lottery. The business model is based on continuous growth. When growth rates fall, the bottom of the pyramid starts to thin out. Customer-acquisition costs soar, while attention and loyalty decline.

The wrong side of the gift economy is that it can easily be used to control and to create monopolies. Microsoft gave its browser away because its primary goal was to overcome Netscape. Sun created Java and dispensed it free to overcome the threat that Microsoft might edge its way from the PC market into the workstation market. In both cases, the companies used their existing dominant market position, and their ability to finance loss-making operations, to lock competitors out of their businesses. In these cases, the gift economy was used illegally. In fact, as U.S. District Court Judge Thomas Penfield Jackson ruled in late 1999, this business method actually violates antitrust laws.

At the end of the day, cash flow is cash flow, and no amount of free goods or booming subscriber lists can camouflage the fact that investors ultimately want a return on their capital.

Prosumers

Consumers also create value in the product. There are no longer any sharp borders between consumers and producers in the open source economy. All products involve services that are necessary for the value. The market is moving toward "consumer offers" instead of products. Consumers and producers are dependant on each other. The producer must earn the respect of the consumers. The consumers participate in both the production and the consumption and become *prosumers*, a concept from business thinker Alvin Toffler.

The producers specify the area and create the rules (operating systems or licenses), while the consumers do the job (programming the product). The consumers work in a way idealistic for the companies they feel solidarity with—a social relationship like buying shampoo only at the Body Shop or ice cream from Ben & Jerry's.

Those who work in these multinational value networks feel solidarity toward the system they work for. We are shifting from a linear economy to a network economy, with new concepts, such as value-creating networks. *Value-creating networks* consist of purposeful cooperation between independent firms along a value-added chain to create competitive advantage. The key concept that drives value-creating networks is the delivery of superior customer value. In contrast, social networks have low emphasis on joint creation because these networks develop along personal, rather than industrial, lines.

Since the industrial revolution, value creation has been described as taking place in a given sequence known as *chains of production* or *value chains*. There is a time and a place for the performance of every task as a link in the chain: extraction of a raw material, its transformation into a product, distribution of the product to the market, and finally, consumption (and the disposal of generated waste). The most salient example is the assembly line. In its time, the idea was revolutionary. The discovery that processes could be broken down into their composite parts and then carried out serially—the right task, in the right order, and at the right time—meant productivity increases in orders of magnitude. According to some researchers, the breakthrough of information technology, and its potential to abolish restrictions in time and space, implies that we are on the way to making linear thinking of this kind obsolete. Using electronic networks, tasks may be accomplished without consideration of space (it does not matter where in the real world the participants are located) and time (everything can be done simultaneously).

As Richard Normann and Rafael Ramirez said in their book *Designing Interactive Strategy: From Value Chain to Value Constellation* (John Wiley and Sons, 1994):

> From this more relevant value constellation perspective, value is co-produced by actors who interface with each other. They allocate the tasks involved in value creation among themselves and to others in time and space, explicitly or implicitly. (…) Co-producers constantly reassess each other, and reallocate tasks according to their new views of the comparative advantage they perceive each other to have.

Now that information is available so quickly, so ubiquitously, and so inexpensively, it is not surprising that everyone is complaining of an excess of information. Nowadays the problem is not information access, but information overload. Nobel prize-winning economist Herbert Simon spoke for us all when he said:

> A wealth of information creates a poverty of attention…What information consumes is rather obvious: It consummates the attention of its recipients. Hence a wealth of information creates the attention efficiently among the overabundance of information sources that might consume it.

The real value produced by an information provider comes in locating, filtering, and communicating what is useful to the consumer. It is no accident that the most popular Web sites belong to the search engines, those devices that allow people to find information that they value and to avoid the rest.

Summary

Open is an old concept in the IT industry. *Open systems* was a popular marketing gimmick in the 1980s, but it made the IT industry aware of the importance of compatibility and connectivity and created a lot of what now are obvious standards.

CHAPTER 5

Network Organizations

* * *

In...post-industrial society, the central problem is...how to organize to make decisions—that is to process information.

HERBERT SIMON, *ADMINISTRATIVE BEHAVIOR*, THIRD EDITION, FREE PRESS, 1976

The single most important issue in open source development is not technical—it's organizational. Eric S. Raymond has pointed out that Linus Torvalds' cleverest and most consequential hack was not the construction of the Linux kernel itself, but rather his invention of the Linux development model. It was unintentional, but natural.

Fresh thinking and innovation are the key drivers of success for modern IT companies. Knowledge of the new media and being comfortable with non-hierarchical ways of working are critical to success in an open source environment.

Linus Torvalds is part of the *Nintendo generation*. They have a different set of assumptions about work than their parents. They thrive on collaboration. Their first point of reference is the Internet. They are driven to innovate and have a mind set of immediacy, requiring fast results.

Torvalds lives in Scandinavia and is accustomed to Scandinavian values. Managers in Scandinavia have their own distinct management style unlike the traditional international sort inherited from military organizations. (There is a reason why large corporations have titles like Chief Executive Officer.) According to the World Economic Forum, Scandinavian management is characterized by human values, a willingness to delegate authority, and placing a strong focus on human resources and staff training.

As we will see in this and the next chapter, both circumstances—the shift in values and the management style—are prerequisite for being successful in the open source and network economy.

Different Types of Networks

A network is not only a technical issue, but the focus is almost always technical. There is a lot of confusion around networks from a nontechnical perspective. There are several types of network organizations. Usually we distinguish among three kinds: *internal*, *stable*, and *dynamic*.

Internal network organizations. Loose associations of assets (employees and property rights) and business units contained within a single company, which subject themselves to market forces. Oil companies will trade internally at market transfer prices or secure outside spot contracts because they find it too expensive to misprice exploration, extraction, refining, or distribution costs.

Stable network organizations. Firms engaged in long-term relationships with external suppliers who bring expertise into the parent company. Participants are typically organized around a single large firm as with auto manufacturing.

Dynamic network organization. The open source model, which consists of more temporary alliances of collaborators and companies with key skills, usually organized around a project. Each unit is independent and collaborates on a specific project or opportunity. In the fashion industry, manufacturers, designers, and retailers frequently use this model. This is the only network organization form we touch upon in this book.

In these types of network organizations, the tie strength varies between network members. While network ties begin at the level of individual pairs, links exist at most levels of granularity, but on a sliding scale. Ties tend to be stronger between pairs than between groups. Also, ties between groups tend to be stronger than those between organizations, industries, and whole societies, respectively. Tie strength diminishes with increasing aggregation. Generally network organizations are defined by elements of structure, process, and purpose.

Structure. Structurally, a network organization combines cospecialized, possibly intangible, assets under shared control. Joint ownership is essential, but it must also produce an integration of assets, communication, and command in an efficient and flexible manner.

Process. Procedurally, a network organization constrains the participating collaborators actions via their roles and positions within the organization, while allowing their influence to emerge or fade with the development or dissolution of ties to others.

Purpose. As decision-making members, collaborators intervene and extend their influence through association. They alter the resource landscape for themselves, their networks, and their competitors and in the process can change the structure of the network itself. A network as an organization must have a unifying purpose to create the need for a sense of identity useful in bounding and marshalling the resources, collaborators, and actions necessary for concluding the strategy and goals of purpose. Without a common purpose, the participants cannot determine either the efficacy or desirability of association, or know whether actions are directed toward cooperative gains.

These three design elements—cospecialized assets, joint control, and collective purpose—distinguish network organizations from centralized organizations, inflexible hierarchies, casual associations, haphazard societies, and mass markets.

Specifically, a network organization has weak internal and external boundaries. Management is less hierarchical, deriving its authority more from expertise than from rank. This, in turn, stems from network output demanding a high degree of intangible, local, or specialized know-how (more on this topic in Chapter 6, "Managing a Virtual Team"). Communication is direct and point-to-point rather than "through channels," while knowledge of emerging problems and opportunities may arrive via multiple loose associations or weak ties.

Resources are specialized and customizable within a given product or service scope, yet they are less vertically integrated—the degree to which ownership and property rights relate with a central office—than their hierarchical counterparts.

Purposeful collaborators within the network may establish ties to other collaborators and organizations to get control for themselves or hinder competitors' attempts to do the same. Tasks are more project- and less functionally driven. This gives shorter production times to more differentiated products.

In a network organization, local concerns are more locally addressed. Local conception also implies a higher degree of local ownership and project incentives, which are more performance driven.

Hierarchy or Collaboration?

Organizational structures are often synonymous with a hierarchical organization. Organizational charts are easy to draw; on paper there are very few problems with moving people around like a chessboard. But this management style poorly describes the reality of open source; in fact, it is completely useless in a network organization.

A network is an organization based on contact and communication between many groups or individuals, who are tightly knit and held together. There are many different structures within a network organization at the same time. But more than a structure, it is a matter of the way you use the organization and a way of behavior.

Network membership thus requires a high degree of trust or commitment between parties. This enables partners to make riskier investments and transfer unfinished goods knowing that disputes from unforeseen events will be handled amicably and equitably.

In hierarchical organizations, assets and resources (employees and property rights) are tightly controlled. In free markets, assets are completely distributed. Open source is a free market of assets and resources.

As we saw in Chapter 2, "Open Source in Business Terms," assets (property rights, at least in Europe) must have an owner. Networks involve multiple owners who exercise their stewardship over a specific subset of total assets. That is, at some point in time, you engage programmers who work with a shared ownership. A leading cause of vertical integration—the degree to which ownership and property rights relate with a central office—is asset or resource specificity. More specific assets permit greater efficiency, but if one owner controls them, the owner can hold up the others for the profits from efficiency by denying access to the rights.

The high cost of purchasing and owning such assets often means that cost reduction is achieved by mass production, using scale to amortize fixed costs. Concentrating ownership, therefore, leads to minimal product differentiation and to homogeneous goods, with Microsoft Office and Windows being shining examples.

It is worth noting that one of the principal concerns of the network literature centers on whether networks represent an intermediate organizational form midway between markets and hierarchies. Substantial evidence suggests that markets and hierarchies do not bracket networks. Hierarchies avoid problems with trust and risk due to hold-up and opportunism by integrating assets they require with a central office. Markets involve few repeat transactions, so talk is cheap, reputations are not held dear, and strategic misrepresentation is commonly assumed. In networks—where intangibles and rapidly applied expertise provide key sources of value—reputations, commitments, and trust become essential.

Networks employ more flexible resources such as greater knowledge—the voluntary nature of an open source project gives in all probability more knowledgeable and experienced collaborators—thus permitting greater niche seeking and customization.

More Definitions

There are many formal definitions of a network. Most are more or less the same, but there are different angles of approach.

> The chief structural characteristic of network organization is the high degree of integration across formal boundaries.

W. E. Baker, "The Network Organization in Theory and Practice," in *Networks and Organizations*, N. Nohria and R. G. Eccles, Editors (Harvard Business School Press, 1993)

> A network is a pattern of social relations over a set of persons, positions, groups, or organizations.

L. D. Sailer, "Structural Equivalence: Meaning and Definition, Computation and Application," *Social Networks*, 1978

These definitions are useful because they emphasize structure and different levels of analysis. A strategic view takes a perspective on goal-directed processes and economic competition. A strategic view considers networks to be:

> ...long term purposeful arrangements among distinct but related for-profit organizations that allow those firms in them to gain or sustain competitive advantage.

C. Jarillo, "On Strategic Networks," *Strategic Management Journal*, 1988

A fourth definition incorporates organic adaptation and flexibility, suggesting networks be:

> ...adapted to unstable conditions, when problems and requirements for action arise which cannot be broken down and distributed among specialists' roles within a hierarchy. ... Jobs lose much of their formal definition ... Interaction runs laterally as much as vertically. Communication between people of different ranks tends to resemble lateral consultation rather than vertical command [and] omniscience can no longer be imputed to the head of the concern.

C. Argyris and D.A. Schon, *Organizational Learning: A Theory of Action Perspective*, Addison-Wesley, 1978

Open Source Networks

Fredrick Brooks, an authority on software engineering, has found that, due to rising costs of coordination, production time increases exponentially with the number of developers.

In the corporate world, Brooks' Law (see Chapter 2 for a more detailed discussion of Brooks' Law) is considered obvious. In the case of Linux, however, there has never been any centralized organization to mediate the communication between Linus Torvalds and all the Linux code contributors. There aren't any project teams with specifically assigned contributors. Each person in the Linux project had the freedom of choice to decide what to work on at the moment.

There are three basic requirements for the success of an open source project:

It is not possible to code from the ground up in open source style. It is possible to test, debug, and improve code in open source style, but a project has never originated in open source mode. The developer community needs to have something that runs from the start that can be tested and played with.

There must be a virtual network that can cooperate. The Internet is the necessary technical network platform, but technology alone is not sufficient. There must also be a virtual network of collaborators. But it is not "the end of hierarchy." In any institution there has to be an authority who can make final decisions. In the Linux case it is Linus Torvalds. In the Apache case it is the Apache team. The Foundation is overseen by a board of directors, who are elected by the Apache Software Foundation membership on an annual basis according to the corporation's bylaws. The board appoints a set of officers to manage the day-to-day operations of the Foundation and oversee the Apache projects. Each project is managed by a self-selected team of technical experts who are active contributors to the project, according to whatever guidelines for collaborative development are best suited to that project.

Most importantly, as all open source development builds on voluntariness, a leader must earn the respect of the collaborators. You can never force anyone to volunteer. The collaborators must find interest in the project and keep this interest over time. This calls for a totally different management style. Open source is doomed to fail inside the traditional, hierarchical, military leadership used in most corporations.

Summary

Network organizations build on nonhierarchical values and a collaborative management style. People participate in open source projects as individuals. To get involved they have to solve problems that they find interesting. If there is a requirement, it means there is a problem that someone else will want to help solve. This also implies that there is no real requirement if no one wants to help solve the problem.

Open source projects are organized as dynamic networks with temporary alliances of collaborators and companies with key skills. A network organization has weak internal and external boundaries. Management is less hierarchical, deriving its authority more from expertise than from rank. This, in turn, stems from network output demanding a high degree of intangible, local, or specialized know-how described in the next chapter, "Managing a Virtual Team."

CHAPTER 6

Managing a Virtual Team

People think just because it is open source, the result is going to be automatically better. Not true. You have to lead it in the right directions to succeed. Open source is not the answer to world hunger.

LINUS TORVALDS, INTERVIEW, *INFOWORLD*, 1999

The only way to manage a virtual team is with trust, respect, and commitment. Forget traditional management theories. (Well, at least some.) Forget business as usual.

Open source changes the organizational pattern and encourages us to alter our perspective on how we manage organizations, how we view and value our employees, and how we approach problems. It is a paradigm shift.

Paradigms are not about technologies or products. They are about a change in perspective. A paradigm defines our basic assumptions about reality. It is the model for our actions. It is not the paradigm that causes change. It is the change itself that forces us to alter our paradigm. Changes of models occur in times of great unrest like today. We are living in a paradigm shift.

The Paradigm Shift

The paradigm shift is neither the open source nor the Internet. The paradigm shift is in our perception of management and business in an open source context. Because open source is such a powerful change agent, understanding the potential paradigm conflicts is an important issue.

In very general terms, the two views in conflict are the organization as a hierarchical system managed by command versus the organization as an organic, self-adapting system managed by trust, performance, and results.

People who work for an organization are assumed to be employees. They are dependent on the organization for their livelihood and their careers. They are also assumed to be subordinates. These assumptions were formulated during the First World War and assumed that the great majority of employees had either no skill or low skills and performed assigned tasks. In a network or open source organization these assumptions are no longer valid.

In the classic industrial organization, decisions are made centrally and filtered down a pyramid of managers, who are trusted to convey, properly interpret, and oversee the implementation.

A network organization, on the other hand, has open boundaries that form a global virtual team. In this book, I define a *network organization* as a group of many different people with different skills, where the members stick together and help each other. It's as simple as that. In the open source context it is often called an *open source community*. A community, or a global virtual team, is a temporary group of people assembled on an as-needed basis for the duration of a task and staffed by voluntary members from virtually anywhere on the Internet.

Network organizations often evolve out of personal or small group connections. Many of the networks already found in the publishing, fashion, computer software, construction, and entertainment businesses, are comprised of individuals, independent production teams, or very small business units. In such teams, coordination is accomplished via mutual trust and a shared communication system.

Distributed decision-making forms the basis of this organic, self-adapting organization. The open source network organization provides the communication capability to coordinate the output of a distributed organization to support goal-directed activities.

A loosely coupled network gives the participants freedom to carry on projects of their own that otherwise couldn't fit in the business concept. These are called *free agents*. An open source project is inherently distributed, where implementation and decisions are mainly the responsibility of each associate, collaborator, or free agent (or whatever the members of the open source network community are called).

General Principles of Organization

There is no such thing as *the one right organization*. Each situation requires a specific organization, with its distinct strengths, limitations, and specific applications. For example, a diocese is not organized the same way as General Motors.

Organization is a tool for productivity in working relationships. As such, a given organization structure fits certain tasks in certain conditions at certain times. Sometimes the best solution is a hierarchy. Other situations may require an organization that facilitates reflection among the workers. Others may require the collective resources in a team. For example, some network organizations may require a strict functional organization with free agents performing tasks for which they are most qualified. Others that involve decision making at an early stage require teamwork from the beginning.

The following are two general principles of organization:

> People must understand the organizational structure in which they are supposed to work.

> There has to be someone who can make final decisions. This is especially important if the project or company is in a crisis. If the ship goes down, the captain does not call for a meeting. Everyone must obey orders, know exactly where to go and what to do, and do it without argument.

Consensus management, as opposed to *hierarchical management*, has often been cited as a prime cause of failure when leading an organization in crises (organizational changes, for example). No one wants to have his or her own job or department cut away to improve the organization as a whole. In times of crisis, consensus management can misallocate resources because it often leads to proportional burden sharing rather than complete restructuring. Consensus management and empowerment change organizational behavior. Once given authority, individuals will fight to extend it. Thus, networks more than hierarchies tend to be the victim of corporate politics. When titular authority yields to expertise, task delegation, which was formerly a matter of command, becomes a matter of persuasion and negotiation.

Shifting between networks and hierarchies has social management consequences. Interpersonal skills come to the fore, and people are free to challenge the authority. Network structures are flexible, but fraught with conflict if not handled properly. For example, any conflict of loyalties is devastating. Having more than one boss immediately creates a conflict. The soundest organization has as few layers as possible.

Network Organizations

There are many different *network* concepts. The first type of network is a technical infrastructure, such as wide area networks, or WAN (the Internet, for example).

The second type is an economical network that shows *network effects*, as we discussed in Chapter 4, "Open Source and the Internet Economy." A *traditional market* is characterized by "decreasing marginal profit." If you were hungry you would probably pay quite a lot for the first meal. But after having eaten, the next meal is not particularly interesting. The same goes for all kinds of capital goods. On the other hand, a *network economy* is characterized by "increasing marginal profits." The value of a network increases exponentially in relation to the number of nodes it contains. When the value of a product to one user depends on how many other users there are, the product displays network effects. Communications technologies are a prime example: Telephones, mobile phones, email, Internet access, fax machines, and modems all exhibit network effects.

Technologies subject to strong network effects tend to exhibit long lead times followed by explosive growth. This pattern results from positive feedback. As the installed base of users grows, it becomes more and more interesting for a single user to adopt the technology. Eventually, the product achieves critical mass and takes over the market. Internet technology was developed in the early 1970s, but didn't really take off until the late 1980s. When Internet traffic finally started to grow, it doubled every year.

But network effects are not restricted to communications networks. They are also powerful in virtual networks, such as the community of Linux users. Each Linux user benefits from a larger network, since this facilitates the exchange of files, programs, and knowledge, and encourages software houses to devote more resources to developing software for the Linux platform.

Because these virtual networks of compatible users generate network effects, popular hardware and software systems enjoy a significant competitive advantage over less popular systems. It is not a matter of quality or of one technology being superior to another. It is simply a matter of one technology being more popular than another, despite its quality or lack of quality.

The third type of network is an organizational network, or business development network. This is the community—the social form of network. An organizational network is a way of cooperating on projects with mutual interests. Organizational networks are a way of gaining creativity and smarter thinking, new perspectives and new competence, as well as creating an extended market and obtaining additional customer references. This type of network builds on trust, respect, and commitment. The tool is the Internet.

It All Depends on Trust

The consequences of the Internet as a social community have been widely debated in networking literature. *Social capital* is the putty that holds a community or group together. Social capital is made up of reciprocal trust between human beings with confidence in each other. This capacity has been shown to be fundamental to the way both democracy and the economy work.

Communities where people tend to trust one another, irrespective of whether or not they are acquainted, are communities with the potential for success. In such communities, people can work together in the marketplace and in politics to create a common good. In these communities, basic trust (the social capital) is firmly in place.

In other societies (developing countries, for example, like the former Soviet Union, which has no experience of a real market), the absence of mutual trust often makes it impossible for people to work together effectively. Instead, time and money go into drawing up agreements, lawsuits, and litigation expenses so people can feel confident that contracts entered into will be respected.

This applies to the real world as well as the virtual community. Political scientist Robert Putnam has demonstrated that it is precisely a social capital deficit that prevents southern Italy from becoming as well developed as northern Italy. Economic historian and Nobel Prize laureate Douglass North uses similar arguments in explaining the differences between wealthy and poor nations.

Putnam claims that social capital is created in the meeting places in a community. People learn to trust one another through repeated successful joint actions.

The Internet is a meeting place, but the question is whether it is possible to achieve a strong enough sense of community there for social capital to be created. In *Trust: The Social Virtues and the Creation of Prosperity* (Free Press, 1995), Francis Fukuyama energetically pursues the thesis that there is a link between reciprocal trust between the members of a community and the ability of that community to achieve economic success. He is skeptical about the potential of the virtual community to create the necessary trust. In his view, the absence of accepted rules and laws, plus the possibility of anonymity, make it altogether too easy to abuse the freedom of the Internet.

Open source advocates believe that networks for enterprises and individuals are a new kind of organization, superior in many ways both to hierarchies and pure market relationships. However, if networks are to prove generally superior to the hierarchical model, there have to be more reciprocal trust and shared norms than there are today, covering what is considered acceptable behavior on the part of network members.

Yet there are researchers—such as Sirkka L. Jarvenpaa at the University of Texas in Austin and Dorothy E. Leidner at Insead in Paris—who have found that social capital can be generated in virtual teams (in virtual companies and political organizations). ("Is Anybody Out There? Antecedents of Trust in Global Virtual Teams." *Journal of Management Information Systems*. Vol. 14, No. 4, Spring 1998.) In their research of social capital on the Internet, they have pointed out the importance of coordinators to create confidence on the part of network participants. When a coordinator can behave in a confidence-inspiring fashion and establish rules for interaction that are acceptable to all, then social capital (or reciprocal trust) can arise and walls of suspicion can be broken down.

The focus of the reported study was to explore the antecedents of trust in a global virtual team setting. Seventy-five teams, consisting of four to six members residing in different countries, interacted and worked together for eight weeks. The two-week trust-building exercises had a significant effect on the members' perceptions of the other members' ability, integrity, and benevolence. In the early phases, team trust was predicted strongest by perceptions of other team members' integrity, and weakest by perceptions of their benevolence. The effect of other members' perceived ability on trust decreased over time. The members' own propensity to trust had a significant, though unchanging, effect on trust. A qualitative analysis of six teams' electronic mail messages explored strategies that were used by the three highest trust teams, but were used infrequently or not at all by the three lowest trust teams. The strategies suggest the presence of *swift* trust.

In a network organization there must be confidence that every associate feels responsible and makes an effort to do high-quality work. Trust is not a certainty; it is but a belief that the associates will assume responsibility and that they have the qualifications and the experience for the task. You know very few people so well that you are fully aware of their skills and personal qualities.

Trust is also based on experience and impression. Usually it is established on how a person presents himself or herself. Only experience shows whether there is justification for this trust. If the person lives up to the trust, it is consolidated. If the person does not live up to the trust, there are distrust and suspicion. A failed relationship can be reestablished, but it is difficult.

Trust is a balance of not knowing for certain, but knowing something about a person's capabilities. The difficult part is to show confidence and to be able to let go of the need to control.

Business Development Networks

There are two ways to build a company. The first is to gather a bunch of people, raise some funding, and start a new firm. The advantage is that you can build capital. The drawback is that the owners can quarrel about assignments and investments, as different people have different preferences at various times. The alternative is to run a business development network in cooperation with several companies or persons.

A company is usually a homogeneous cultural and communication circle. That's why *corporate culture* is a well-known concept. But that is not always desirable, especially in knowledge companies. Creativity builds on manifoldness and is critical to a company's long-term survival. Without the development of a creative environment within the organization, companies will be trapped within the model of their existing business and will not be able to adapt to the needs and changes in the outside world.

It is prerequisite that creative environments are created through a secure economical base together with free time (free as in liberty, not as in free beer). This gives people the opportunity to reflect on issues other than daily supplies. A university, college, or research institute provides this economic base—most scientists and researchers have freedom of research, but are paid. They have the time to create international networks and create contact with other cultures. They have informal meeting places—lists, news groups, chats—where spontaneous discussions can take place on mutual topics that cross social, ethnical, and professional boundaries.

A network organization consists of an *inner core* or *spider* (the boss) that controls and drives the network. It could be a person like Linus Torvalds, or a group with a goal or joint strategy, together with an understanding of the core competence of the organization. The inner core or spider manages the marketing, as well as sales and delivery of products.

The core can temporarily engage suppliers and producers as needed and the network can expand or reduce as required. The number and size of the tasks determine who participates in the network at a certain time. The growth and renewal of the network take place due to the inner core's active interest in finding new opportunities. Therefore, the expectation is high on activity and personality.

According to Lone Dalsgaard and Jan Bendix in their book *Network Organization*, (PriceWaterhouseCoopers/Uppsala Publishing House, 1998), a network organization has six characteristics, which we'll discuss in turn in the following sections:

> Formulated values
> Decentralization
> Multiple leaders' roles
> Flexible organizational boundaries
> Interdependence
> Transparency

Formulated Values

Formulated values are common values including norms, morals, and ethics that form the basis for an associate's performance. These values must be clear and accepted by everyone, as participation is voluntary. Associates know the boundaries and know how to act within them; thus, the need for management and control is reduced.

Formulated values give the associates a guidance tool. Formulated values, together with intelligent management, allow collaborators to act in the project and learn to have trust in the process.

Decentralization

The network organization divides large projects into smaller units or builds the organization around small units from the start. Many associates are given influence and responsibility, which results in increased commitment.

Multiple Leaders' Roles

Managers in a network organization are not placed on a hierarchical ladder on the way to the top; there are many new managerial roles. Each associate has several managers, and the managerial roles are distributed in such a way that you can be a manager for a person in one situation and vice versa in another. Associates lead each other.

Flexible Organizational Control

The network organization has few internal boundaries, and the interfaces to suppliers and customers, for example, are flexible and open. The collaborators use each other as well as external partners for mutual exchange of information and knowledge.

Interdependence

The collaborators in a network organization recognize and acknowledge their dependence on each other and on associates and competitors outside the organization.

Transparency

Free flow of information is necessary for success. Uninformed people cannot take responsibility, whereas informed people cannot avoid taking responsibility. Every action and control mechanism around the project must be transparent so that all information is available to everyone in the project.

In the classic industrial organization, power is wielded by hoarding information. In the open source culture, value is placed on sharing information. Managers who have built their careers by carefully controlling and restricting the flow of information find it difficult to grasp the value of an intranet, and look for both reasons and technologies to restrict and control its content.

An organization whose culture values employees for their ability to follow routines rather than for their knowledge and experience, and that does not trust employees to act in the company's interest, should not implement an open source culture.

Global Virtual Teams

In order for a network organization to be successful, it must have open boundaries and many communication lines. Network organizations can be used both within large companies or organizations, and as an organizational form between companies and/or persons.

The advantage of a network organization is that it can fulfill the demands of the current assignment and morph concurrently with changes in the environment. A network organization is flexible enough to adapt to conditions quickly. It is a prerequisite to have free and independent associates who are able to take initiative and be mobile.

Such an organization cannot be drawn in boxes. Instead it's a network of projects, ensuring that individuals are displayed within the projects basic ideas and fulfilling the project's goals with room for individuality (not just adjustment). A network organization grows through the optimum effort of the individual.

A network organization applied inside a large company also facilitates the development of the employees. Therefore, a network is a way to become both larger and smaller at the same time, with no extra cost. Keeping the organization small or retaining the small units in order to maintain efficiency improve quality and increase the associates' influence and responsibility. Thus, the company can grow in scope rather than in size. The associates build on each other's resources, preserve the small and clear format, independence, and distinctive character, but make the most of the solidarity and the inspiration from others. At the same time, they keep a distance and avoid a financial dependence, but exchange experience and knowledge.

A network of companies can favor many parts, as the sum of the parts is larger than each part separately. For example: A mediates business to B in the network. On another occasion it is the opposite. Agreement can generate cheaper purchases due to large-scale effects. A network can compensate for lack of resources in one node, which is cheaper and easier than hiring more people.

All individuals in the network must:

➤ Trust each other and have the ability to create confidence.

➤ Have a sense of leadership responsibility. It is important to not look upon the network as a personal asset (this leads to selfishness) but as an asset for the group. It is important as an individual to feel the teamwork and know one's role.

➤ Have the ability to cooperate fairly in the working team.

➤ Have pedagogical talent and be able to convey ideas to new partners in order to officially represent the team and its values.

➤ Be generous, unbiased, and able to share information and ideas without demanding any compensation. All individuals must contribute to the development of the organization.

NOTE

It is not possible to demand participation in all projects. Projects belong to those who implement ideas.

A network can be looked upon in three conceptual metaphors: the network (1) as a computer, (2) as an economy, and (3) as a community. These three metaphors draw on established principles of decision processes, rational agency, and of organizational behavior to help judge the different architectural models.

Briefly, the computer metaphor models the firm as a decision process dependent on management capabilities, communication paths, utilization rates, and decision errors while minimizing the costs of decision resources. Persons interested in decision efficiency can engage the computer metaphor, for example, to examine why shifting the focal point of decisions changes throughput, errors, and communication costs.

The economic metaphor leads to the question of how to motivate self-interested parties to achieve mutually satisfactory results. Efficiency is maximized when redistributing a trade surplus leaves everyone at least as well off as before. All associates are at all times assumed to behave rationally and purposefully with respect to their own welfare. The purpose of collaboration is to produce a surplus at least as great as the sum of agents' gains working independently. Processes typically seek to align incentives in decentralized systems, to create and capture consumer surplus, and to establish mechanisms through which agents truthfully reveal their hidden information.

The computer and economic metaphors are often questioned. Social patterns of human interaction exceed the simplified economic model. The pursuit of economic goals is typically accompanied by such noneconomic goals as sociability, approval, status, and power. Economic action is socially situated and cannot be explained by reference to individual motives alone. Thus, market-pricing models appear to simplify the human mechanisms and fail to capture the intricacies and richness of responsive human interaction.

Thus, the community metaphor augments the computer and economy metaphors by focusing on human context. It concerns human response to contextual cues such as different types of boundaries, cultural or structural behavior constraints, communication styles, and content. This approach recognizes the mechanisms influenced by desires for power and recognition, fear of shame, and avoidance of demeaning work among others.

Network organizations are ineffective at first glance. According to research findings (for example, H. J. Leavitt's *Unhuman Organizations* published in the Harvard Business Review, 1962), two basic results emerged from experimenting in a different organizational structure. First, according to measurable efficiency criteria such as speed, message count, and careful use of resources, the centralized structure outperformed the network structure on almost all tasks. The network lacked a central coordinating mechanism and spent more time negotiating procedures.

On the other hand, however, persons in the network structure were inclined to value their participation more and were much happier with their experience. (The one exception was the head of the hierarchy, who was generally quite unhappy with his subordinate experience.)

Second, for the more abstract tasks, the network tended to generate more innovative ideas, which were also adopted more frequently. New ideas generated in the centralized configuration were more likely to be discarded on the grounds that the central person was too busy, that the innovation was too bothersome to implement, or that current practices required no improvement.

Lead Rather Than Manage

One does not manage people.

The task is to lead people.

And the goal is to make productive the specific strengths and knowledge of each individual.

Peter F. Drucker, *Management Challenges for the 21st Century,*
HarperCollins, 1999

In a network organization people are not employees. They are associates working for the organization. This is the situation in most knowledge companies, like consulting firms. They know more about their job than their boss or anybody else in the organization.

These associates are dependent on their boss when it comes to being engaged, appraised, and so on. But the boss can only perform if the associates take responsibility for their work and for making the boss understand what the work and the result of the work mean. Based on this information the boss then decides on a direction. The associate is dependent on the boss to define what the "score" is for the entire organization, and the standards, values, performance, and results.

The relationship between the boss and the associate in a network organization is more like the relationship between a conductor and the musicians in an amateur orchestra. The musicians are engaged voluntarily and are free to leave at any time without penalty. These relationships are based on trust. Just as an orchestra can sabotage even the most competent conductor, an autocratic conductor cannot keep annoyed musicians. You must earn respect. It cannot be forced. As Eric S. Raymond phrased it in "The Cathedral and the Bazaar":

If you're writing for the world, you have to listen to your customers—this doesn't change just because they're not paying you in money.

Associates in a network organization need to be managed as volunteers or equal partners. They are paid, but they are free to leave at any time. They own their "means of production," which is their knowledge.

Open source is based on a meritocracy, that is, the incentive is merit, rather than money. Money alone does not motivate performance; in fact, dissatisfaction with money grossly demotivates. Money is often a prerequisite for motivation, but in open source it is has no significance. Open source collaborators need a challenge. They need to recognize and believe in the organization's mission. In a technical meritocracy, one makes a career in a network by exhibiting appropriate merit (as a developer, project leader, speaker, or writer). Those who give the most valuable efforts to the network are generally afforded the greatest respect in the network.

Because of its distributed nature, information management in an open source perspective focuses on collecting and communicating "state" information. Distributed decision making leads to *modular organizations*, which means that the processes within the organizational modules are less important than the state of the output. Success becomes a function of successfully managing the states of the organization and its independent modules rather than the processes inside each module.

Managing an open source team must consider and resolve these questions: What does the other party want? What are its values? What are its goals?

Open source encourages distributed decision making, modular organizations, open communication, and application of knowledge. Today, most management openly espouses these platitudes. Be aware that implementing these platitudes, even with the help of an intranet, will likely raise some difficult management challenges that will test your commitment at many points along the way. When this happens, it might be useful to stop and ask yourself: Do I want to engineer every aspect of my organization like a machine or have it respond like an adaptive organism? Do I need an assembly line or a learning organization?

Open Management and Cultural Importance

A common theory of social behavior suggests that groups benefit individuals by providing information resources, emotional resources, and identity support. In turn, groups benefit organizations by coordinating joint activities, promoting specialization, and facilitating organizational learning.

Aside from collective productivity, groups concern themselves with identity maintenance where recognition, fear of shame, and peer pressure play a role. Members tend to judge actions for consistency with identity, using peer pressure to sanction behaviors that challenge group norms (the nail that sticks up is the one hammered down).

Japanese companies pursue extracurricular group activities to socialize employees and establish group identity. These same forces help explain decreased employee morale during layoffs. When group integrity and identity are destroyed, the organization as a community suffers.

Informal cultural constraints can also impact the group in a larger social context. Western traditions regarding personal and religious freedom have led to laws promoting individual rights. The establishment of individual opportunity, for example, extends to legal proscriptions on nepotistic hiring.

In Asian economies, on the other hand, traditions regarding the importance of family and societal obligation have given rise to different expectations regarding loyalty and employment. Despite their size, Korean *chaebol* are essentially family-run businesses. In Japan, keiretsu are descended from family-owned *zaibatsu*, which were forcibly decontrolled after World War II. The same phenomenon holds in Taiwan where *jituanqiye* or family-owned conglomerates play a central role in the economy. With the subordination of individual identity, powerful group-centered organizations emerge.

Psychological theories of social groups tend to view individual behavior in social communities as magnified versions of individual phenomena—in other words, the group behaves as the individuals do. The direction of influence runs from individuals to communities. In contrast, holistic theories consider the direction of influence to be reversed. According to this view, communities have autonomous needs, goals, and interests such that they mold the behaviors of the associates.

Social systems are ongoing and reciprocal patterns of relationships, structures, generative rules, and resources. Within network organizations, identification with group and social norms can guide action even as actions can influence norms. Social structure may be a common law, language, and currency—a uniform way of doing business. In essence, social norms become a substitute for formal controls even as behaviors establish appropriate norms.

It is of no coincidence that open source has been very successful in Scandinavia. Various surveys have shown that especially in Sweden a new generation has emerged that is exceptionally curious, self-reliant, contrarian, smart, focused, able to adapt, high in self-esteem, and globally oriented, having a healthy critical attitude toward authority. Open source projects require individuals to adapt and respond to the needs and attitudes of the group.

The defining characteristic of the *Nintendo generation* is that they are the first to come of age in the Internet era. They have a different set of assumptions about work than their parents have. They thrive on collaboration, and many find the notion of an authoritarian boss somewhat bizarre. They are driven to innovate and have a mind-set of immediacy, requiring fast results. These attributes, combined with the ease of digital tools, spell trouble for traditional enterprises and managers. This generation will pressure for radical changes in existing companies.

The following characteristics of Scandinavian management highlight important open source management objectives:

> Willingness to delegate authority

> Strong focus on human resources and staff training

> Engagement of competent financial and marketing officers

> Short power distances between managers and coworkers

> Informal group relations and work environment

> Open and straightforward communications

> Focus on managing through values and visions

These traditional values are perfectly matched with the network organizations in Internet-based companies. The Scandinavian Airlines' (SAS) focus on the front-line employees and the "turning up-side down of the pyramids" in the SAS organization, gave an echo all over the world in the 1980s of how focus on the employee can generate positive results.

Flat Organizations and Short Power Distance

In industrial society, positions of power are generally limited by geography. For example, a factory owner is the boss in his community, and the chairman of the town council holds the reins of his municipality. These individuals impact decisions made, and bring influence to bear in their geographical arena.

What happens to this kind of geographically based power when more and more important decisions are made in global networks?

Geographically-based institutions and organizations founded on hierarchy lose power in a network organization. With whom shall the CEO of General Motors negotiate? Players who coordinate their work in constantly changing network systems become difficult to contact as counterparts in negotiations, and cannot easily be held accountable for decisions.

Power distance is defined as "the extent to which people in a hierarchical situation feel they can and should control the behavior of others, and the extent to which those others are conditioned by reflexes of obedience." In *flat organizations*, the power distance is largely replaced by personal responsibility.

How the W3C Works: Inside a Distributed Open Source Organization

The W3C is in many ways the prototype for an open source business, yet it is not a business in itself. It is a university-hosted industry consortium. Its resources come from membership fees and a small amount of government funding, but essentially it is a coalition of free agents working together to further the goal of Tim Berners-Lee, the man who invented the World Wide Web, to bring the Web to its full potential.

What that potential is, and even what the Web is, is a constant source of debate. That debate, and the debate around any specification that the consortium develops, is one of the sources of its vitality, and also its problems.

The W3C develops specifications and software to demonstrate them. The specifications are developed by part-time staff from member organizations. Members of the staff of the W3C, however, develop the software. Companies are often unwilling to provide resources for open-source development, as this goes against the grain of their development process as well as their commercial way of working.

The W3C is an open organization. This means that it encourages the participation of all organizations and individuals who can contribute substantively to specifications, focuses on achieving group consensus among peers, and works to ensure the timely delivery of high-quality technical specifications that have undergone public review. All W3C recommendations are public, and their ultimate success relies upon the voluntary adoption and implementation by the public.

To understand how the W3C operates, it is important to look at its rules for partnering with other organizations. In order to promote architectural consistency between technologies developed within the W3C and those developed by other organizations writing specifications for information technologies, W3C created a process for forming partnerships with these organizations. To prevent market fragmentation, W3C coordinates the development of technologies that are similar to, but is not interoperable with, technologies developed by the W3C.

Another instance is when the partnership would mean the application of a W3C technology to a new domain. The goal of such a partnership would be to promote deployment of W3C technologies and understand requirements from new domains.

Finally, coordination is considered when the partnership means the development of complementary technologies. This type of partnership would help resolve mutual dependencies.

Partnerships are likely to vary from organization to organization, so the goals and processes described are designed to be flexible. They will be refined as W3C learns from experience. What makes a partnership possible reflects the rules and principles of the W3C. When a partnership is considered, the W3C requests that the partner agrees to make public process and membership information. This includes a publicly documented position on its membership and partnership policies that permits widespread participation of all interested parties within its scope of activity. The W3C declines to partner with organizations that have selective or arbitrary membership policies that serve only to benefit preexisting or dominant member organizations.

Another principle that is important to the W3C is the process of consensus decision. Groups operating within a partnership agree to reach consensus in order to provide a single solution acceptable to both partners and the market at large. Where unanimity is not possible, minority opinions are archived. Another important position is that specifications are widely available and free of charge. In practice, this means publishing them on the Web and keeping them accessible for the life of the organization. A partner agrees to allow its peers to archive/mirror specifications and also to make them available, with clear attribution of the source, in the event the organization cannot. The organization archives all discussion and input to its work, as well as the specification. This is required for the peer review process to work well. When specifications are distributed, any publications resulting from the joint effort should carry the W3C document notice, as well as distribute any software resulting from the joint effort according to the W3C IPR software notice.

Peer review, an important feature of the scientific process, and as such also important to the W3C as an open source organization, is required for the creation of a partnership. A partner agrees to have joint work reviewed by peers at appropriate/documented milestones to ensure compatibility and likewise to review the work of peers. The partner agrees to negotiate changes deemed necessary by reviewers. But review does not stop with peer review. To enable a truly open process (as Eric Raymond has said, "given enough eyeballs, all bugs are shallow"), the review process must be public, as well. The partner agrees to solicit and respond to comments made during periods of public review. This does not mean giving up all secrets, however. The W3C requires partners to respect the confidentiality of sensitive information shared within a Working Group. Willingness by all parties to protect such information is said to foster trust and may allow Working Groups to get work done more quickly. However, it is clearly stated that those involved should not lose sight of the ultimate goal of open and public specifications.

The W3C has a preference for specifications that are unencumbered by intellectual property rights claims (for instance, patent claims). Where such claims exist, public disclosures should be made as early as possible. Technology devel-

continues

How the W3C Works: Inside a Distributed Open Source Organization (Continued)

oped within the partnership must be available to the public under reasonable and nondiscriminatory licensing terms.

Another requirement is softer: The W3C requires the partner's mission to promote the technical, institutional, or social evolution and interoperability of distributed information systems—for instance, open source development. This also includes coordinating all public statements and press releases related to the joint effort.

Joint work with the partner will be carried out in a single Working Group, when the work falls with the charter of that Working Group, or a Coordination Group, when the work spans several Working Groups.

Both W3C and the partner must have access to a joining partnership agreement, and this document must be available on the Web with appropriate access rights.

The W3C develops recommendations to its members; it is not a formal standards body, and it does not have legislative powers. If anyone does not want to implement a recommendation, it is their choice. But it is the members who develop the specifications, and it is they who are the main resource of the organization. The specification work is conducted in Working Groups, open to any member who wants to commit the requisite resources. Members commit the time of their staffers to the W3C, to produce recommendations.

When W3C decides to become involved in an area of Web technology or policy, it initiates an Activity in that area. An Activity means that W3C resources—people, time, money, and so on—are dedicated to work in that area.

An Activity is created as follows: The Director proposes an Activity to the Advisory Committee in a call for review that includes a reference to a defining briefing package. To create an Activity, the organizers of the Activity propose a briefing package to the W3C management group (W3M), consisting of the members of the W3C staff that are managers of the different areas within the W3C (Technology and Society, Architecture, User Interface, and Web Accessibility Initiative), plus a few members of the administrative staff, and some former domain managers, whose position corresponds to that of area directors in the IETF. If the W3M group approves the proposal, the Director proposes the Activity to the Advisory Committee (which consists of one representative from each member organization). After review by the Advisory Committee, the Director announces the disposition of the proposal.

The advantage of being an open source organization is simply the ability to get better quality work done more quickly. W3C is one of the best examples of a successful open source organization. It's operations are global and international, it uses the Internet heavily, and the value of the organization increases as the knowledge collected among voluntary contributors is freely shared at no cost.

Flat organizations have a team-oriented structure with few management levels. The result is a simple and direct decision-making process. In a flat team-oriented organization, a manager is a coach rather than a commander, and often entrusts tasks and authority to his staff. In flat organizations, employees on all levels have the freedom to make decisions and solve unexpected problems without asking superiors for permission.

The traditional power elite like corporate executives are losing influence in the network society. More anonymous forces are taking power. It is easy to name the people who are losing power, but not quite so easy to identify those who are gaining it.

Networks are fundamentally about interplay, where no individual can be held accountable. On the other hand, power is more evenly distributed in a network than in a hierarchy. The truly virtual enterprise is a company without a hierarchy. In that sense, a network implies a more democratic system than the traditional hierarchical society.

Summary

Knowledge-based companies have their value in volatile assets: the employees. The employees are free to leave the company at any time. Open source networks consist of virtual teams of volunteers. In such an organization, this inherent volatility is carried to an extreme. Thus, an open source team can only be managed by two mechanisms: trust and respect. Neither can be bought or forced. Trust can only be created and respect can only be earned. How this is done is discussed in the next chapter.

CHAPTER 7

Managing Distributed Open Source Projects

Why does free love cost so much?

GRAFFITI

Most open source projects have up until now been driven by enthusiasm and hard work. A professional exploitation of the open source development methods demands a systematic approach. Managing an open source project requires different demands on management and leadership.

As our society and businesses become more complex and distributed, there is a greater need to manage projects across time and space. The Web now provides a less expensive way to transfer information and collaborate in a distributed manner. It is no surprise that many large organizations and vendors of collaborative tools see a great opportunity for these technologies to be applied to manage distributed projects.

However, this increased need for collaboration cannot be satisfied by technology alone. There are substantial changes in behavior that are required, and there are key driving trends in technology, culture, infrastructure, and performance opportunities that we need to understand before we can deal effectively with the challenges of collaboration and distributed project management.

As the world's economies become more interconnected, and more competitive, there is an increasing need for organizations to form joint design and manufacturing teams that collaborate for the life of a project and then disperse.

Internet-based tools, services, protocols, and design methodologies allow contractors to compose teams of specialists from different locations and organizations as project needs arise.

For almost a half century the IT industry has consistently failed to deliver the necessary computer applications on time and within budget or to provide the functionality needed by the business. It has taken 40 years to understand that business requirements change rapidly and are difficult to define, and that the people who understand business processes best are the people who use them day to day.

It is interesting to note that most IT projects are overdue and overrun project budget. According to a recent report by the Standish Group, 30 to 45 percent of systems projects fail before completion, over 50 percent of IT projects overrun budgets and schedules by 200 percent or more, and failed systems projects cost over $100 billion per year. In addition, only 16 percent of software projects are on time and on budget in small to midsize companies and an even lower 9 percent in large companies. Also, projects completed by large American companies have only 42 percent of the originally proposed features and functions, and 48 percent of IT executives feel that there are more failures currently than just five years ago.

Development projects can gain a life of their own and become trapped in their own complexity. There have been a number of serious attempts to understand the application development process and to codify ways in which these failures can be overcome.

Simply by showing extraordinary results, open source has become one of the best development methods available. The problem is that contrary to other development methods, it doesn't have any underlying theories. It just works.

Sound application development is mostly a matter of managing a project. Application development is not a black art and is amenable to structure and discipline.

Given that we are building business systems with some IT content, the fundamental principles behind open source development are simple—they are essentially the same as in any other development project:

Development is a team effort. It must combine the members' knowledge of the business requirements with the technical skills of IT professionals.

High quality demands fitness for purpose as well as technical robustness. Build the right product before you build it right. Developers should not get bogged down in delivering technically refined solutions. Some technical issues can be left until later, if the operational characteristics are sufficiently robust in the short term. Traditionally, the focus of developers has been on satisfying all the requirements in a theoretical specification. It may well be that the requirements are inaccurate or unnecessary.

Development can be incremental. Not everything has to be delivered at once, and delivering something earlier is often more valuable than delivering something later.

The law of diminishing return applies. Resources must be spent developing the features of most value to the members.

The Open Source Team

An Open Source Team is a small number of people with competence that complement each other, that works towards a joint purpose, target and line of action, and support mutual responsibilities for the performance of the team.

Bo Gahm, CEO, Strategic Management Training, Sweden

Managing a distributed open source project is about managing a team of people. It is truly understanding the members' needs, making them deliver solutions that work, and delivering them as quickly and as cheaply as possible.

Open source will certainly not solve every IT problem, but it will go a long way toward ensuring that the business gets the application systems it needs.

In the past, project managers in various industries have employed a variety of planning and control methodologies as well as tools to support them, but with mixed results. There are many project management methodologies, lots of standards and organizations supposedly proven "best practices," yet still there is a low percentage of successful IT projects. The reality is that project work is difficult, and in most cases, less than successful from an organizational and business perspective.

What makes success? Do successful projects have certain characteristics? If so, what characteristics are key, and is it even feasible to effectively lead and manage geographically distributed work efforts?

Specific behaviors can and should be applied to managing projects in a distributed environment such as open source. The current wave of technological advances provides useful tools that enable us to achieve higher project success rates more consistently.

Network or Virtual Organization?

Open source as an application development method is basically managing a bunch of scattered voluntary developers in a project. To be practically manageable the team needs some kind of organization and management.

By definition the open source team forms a *virtual* or *network organization*. (The difference between the two forms is still debated among researchers. In this book I do not distinguish between the two.) To utilize the business opportunities in this form of organization, the aim of the network is simply to achieve market differentiation by performing better. The company can obtain all noncritical competencies and activities from outside (that is, from other members in the team with which it forms a network organization). Furthermore it aims to improve competitiveness and productivity, to enhance efficiency and responsiveness, and decrease overheads.

What advantages does a network organization have over ordinary strategic alliances, joint ventures, or other forms of collaboration? At what point do critical success factors differ for network organizations and other forms of collaboration? Or is it just a loose grouping?

And is managing a network organization truly so different from managing, for example, an alliance? Is a network organization finished the moment participants decide to establish contracts? If so, where are the borders and how relevant is it to define those borders?

The main difference is the technology. *Network* surely means an electronic network where people are wired together and therefore have access to information online. A joint venture or any other form of collaboration may simply be a group of people getting together face-to-face.

The main differences between a network organization and other forms of cooperation are that a network gives:

➤ Contribution of core competencies only

➤ Entrepreneurial independence

➤ High flexibility

Also, partners can unite quickly, with no lengthy negotiations, partnerships can disband without any problems, and a member or company can be a partner of several network organizations.

An important additional benefit of open source teams, if they are working at different times at different locations, is that it allows people more time to think and respond coherently. Leaders are often skilled verbally and quick thinkers. Others need more time to ponder, contemplate, and work through the argument.

Principal Differences

People are key to successful work in network organizations. When people are separated geographically from each other, they must work more autonomously and be prepared to make decisions independently. They must also work in collaboration with distant colleagues who may have vastly different experiences, perspectives, and incentives. The success of the open source environment is dependent on the expertise, knowledge, and wisdom of individuals.

Working in an open source team is a very different experience from working face-to-face. The principal issues are the lack of face-to-face contact, difficulties of disambiguating communication, feelings of isolation, and difficulties in trusting other team members. Skills and competencies, including leadership, gained in the face-to-face environment do not necessarily transfer to the open source environment.

One particular issue for team leaders is to determine the necessary communication tool needed for different types of communication. Too many team leaders think that email is the only tool needed. Email is not necessarily good for all leadership communications.

In the traditional environment, communication and information access occurs in a shared context, but in a open source environment it occurs between individuals in a number of different physical contexts. A number of critical interrelated areas are impacted as work is conducted in varied physical contexts. These areas must be explicitly managed for successful implementation of open source work.

When performing work activities in an open source environment, individuals access information and communicate with colleagues from a variety of different physical locations. This differs significantly from the traditional office, where individuals work at a single location. In a traditional office, interaction between colleagues takes place through face-to-face contacts in both formal meetings and informal settings.

However, in open source environments people work at different geographical locations and often at different times, for example, telecommuting. In order to communicate and coordinate these activities, individuals use a variety of non-face-to-face communication channels. These channels include electronic communication modes such as fax, email, shared on-line databases, and traditional modes such as paper memos, notes, telephone, and voicemail.

Telecommuting research indicates that certain skills are necessary to be effective in this context, for example, time management and self-supervisory skills.

Managers of telecommuters must address employee development issues such as the potential loss of visibility for workers leading to reduced promotion and development opportunities. It is of vital importance that managers know the difference between guiding and supervising, and controlling and observing.

Relationship Management

In open source, management of work becomes more complex. Work management involves two dimensions:

➤ Management of the processes necessary to perform the work

➤ Management of the execution of these processes

Work processes may have to be redesigned for effective performance in the open source environment.

Relationships are critical for efficient organizational performance as employees perform work activities in a web of social relationships. Knowledge is transferred from one worker to another, new skills are learned, and work activities are coordinated through these relationships. In order to be effective, relationships must be developed with a level of shared expectations and trust between individuals.

Relationships between individuals are particularly critical in a network organization. It is important to develop common understanding and trust among all participants. This web of trust is critical, as open source management processes must be conducted at a level of openness that historically has not existed between developers and vendors, who typically battle each other continually about price and availability of product. Development of relationships in an open source environment appears more difficult as individuals are working in a different context, and the development of a shared understanding of information and communication patterns is less easily achieved.

In addition, informal social communication, which is important for the development of working relationships, is less likely to happen naturally when people do not work within walking distance.

The reduction in informal communication and its impact on working relationships are concerns in telecommuting programs, as managers often fear that employees will be less able to work effectively in teams and that relationships between team members will suffer when workers are geographically separated. This is usually not true. Various studies in Sweden show that the opposite is true. If telecommuters work with tasks that they feel are meaningful, they will work more responsibly and create more quality results. Telecommuters rarely cheat; on the contrary, people frequently accept unpaid overtime when they feel satisfied that they are doing high-quality work.

Trust and Respect

A traditional open source project is characterized by people working together at different times in different places. Open source teams are usually outside a company, but in large corporations they can be in-house. As open source builds on voluntaries, it is essential to build trust and respect. Trust is built in the physical meeting between people, which cannot easily be compensated by computer-aided tools.

The success of open source teams depends largely on building and maintaining trust between the team members. Trust is crucial because it is the defining feature of an open source project.

An open source team is an example of a boundaryless community that has members' affiliations across geography, organizations, and functions. Members mainly interact electronically, with work and services being carried out over a distance and at varying times. There are several reasons for the rapid creation of open source teams.

Specifically, teams may be distributed because of the new realities facing present-day organizations. For example, with emerging markets in different locations, open source teams can increase the span of communication and maximize the level of member participation. Thus, open source teams in a network organization are a strategy for organizational success. Unlike conventional teams, open source teams transcend distance, time zones, and organizational boundaries differing in membership characteristics. However, both teams value relationships, build member identification, and encourage interaction.

While open source teams present great opportunities, their viability and effectiveness also must be evaluated. It is argued that trust may not be possible in open source teams. However, many investigations suggest that trust can exist within open source teams. Contact and interaction have been observed to be the main factors for the existence of trust.

In an open source team social control is based on self-direction and self-control. Collaborative work requires trust and a shared communication system. Most people agree that a successful open source project requires trust between the team members. For example, trust has been identified as an important aspect of interpersonal relationships. Although trust is important in any team, it is essential in an open source team. Collaboration and cooperation is necessary between all stakeholders in the team, otherwise the project quickly becomes "us against them"—an attitude counter to the open source philosophy of shared responsibilities.

This view of trust is based on calculations that weigh the cost and benefits of certain courses of action between members. The social perspective centers on the view of moral duty and shared common values.

In the study "The Role of Trust in Virtual Teams" by Tanko Ishaya and Linda Macaulay (Department of Computation, University of Manchester Institute of Science and Technology, UK), the difference between Web-based shared workspace and desktop videoconferencing is scrutinized. The investigation revealed that computer-based communication destroys trust in virtual teams without the parties concerned being aware that it is happening. It has the capability not only to destroy trust between people but also among whole groups and organizations. Factors that play a part in destroying trust include: flaming, making unreasonable demands of people, imposing work on people, ignoring requests, badmouthing, and failure to meet commitments. Although these things go on in everyday face-to-face interaction between people, in face-to-face communication, there are many things that one would not say to another, whereas, in open source communication people go on criticizing others for a long period and say things they wouldn't have said face-to-face. There is no microfeedback loop providing social constraints in open source communication. However, it was observed that with time trust deepens or retreats based on individual expectations and experiences, which also influences group performance.

Although participation was initially based on self-interest, this was suspended in some groups. Thus, two basic characteristics emerged as relationships changed with time. While there may be other reasons and factors that facilitate performance, there is a clear link between trust and performance. Groups who trust their members have high performance, whereas distrusted memberships have low performance. Trust is seen to confer important advantages on exchange partners.

However, this raises a number of questions and concerns. First, it is important to know whether it can be developed within an electronic environment and if so, how? Also, if it is possible to build, how do we maintain and expand it? Finally, how do we recognize real trust and distinguish it from simulated trust.

The study "The Role of Trust in Virtual Teams," done at the Department of Computation, University of Manchester Institute of Science and Technology, UK, shows the difference in trust between teams who used Web-based shared workspace versus desktop videoconferencing. Basically trust was created if team members were communicative and had a collaborative and cooperative approach. Groups whose members trust each other have high performance, whereas distrusted memberships have low performance, as shown by the results in Table 7.1.

Table 7.1 Results from the Study "The Role of Trust in Virtual Teams"

TRUST DEEPENS	TRUST RETREATS
• Communication was frequent, so members were well informed and shared their understandings.	• There was little communication between members, so ideas were not shared.
• Messages were precategorized, which provided timely responses from each member.	• Members were not responsive, messages that required urgent reply were ignored.
• Tasks were clearly identified, so members knew group objectives.	• Goals were not properly identified.
• Members kept to schedules and deadlines.	• Members did not keep to schedules and deadlines.
• Constant positive feedback was provided, so members had positive reinforcements.	• There was little or no positive feedback provided, so members had no positive reinforcements.
• Members were supportive of one another.	• Members were looking for excuses for not participating rather than making contributions.
• Individuals' and groups' expectations were identified.	• Individuals' and groups' expectations were not identified.
• Members were seen to be very committed and kept their promises.	• Members were not seen to be committed.

There is always the need to build and maintain trust in any working team. Open source communication should be used to build and maintain this trust, not to destroy it. This is obviously a difficult task.

Open source communication either in the form of electronic mail or electronic discussion forums plays a major role in helping to build a knowledge sharing culture. It also has, however, the power to destroy or seriously damage relationships. If you receive and exchange many electronic messages from colleagues each day, you may have experienced this problem. You may be under pressure, and receive more messages than you have time to deal with. It is worst if these messages are unstructured, imposing demands, and if you have to communicate with people whom you have never met, who have different native languages, and who have different cultural backgrounds and many constraints that you are unaware of. Then electronic communication may not only be less effective as a medium for communication but also destroys the knowledge-sharing culture that you are striving to build.

While appreciating the difficulty in building and maintaining trust in open source teams, we are of the view that trust can be built and maintained. Factors and processes that play a role in building this trust are described and presented. We were, however, limited because our conclusions were based on observations and results from only a lab-based case study. Further research is needed to validate these findings. Nevertheless, the lessons learned so far can facilitate greater success in developing trust in an open source team.

In building relations between people, real time does have an advantage. A tool that can easily transfer a large amount of information builds a relation— a smiley cannot compensate for talking to the face of the real person.

What is missing in an open source organization is the effectiveness of communication. This occurs because of the following factors:

There is less communication. I am reluctant to type to the same degree I can verbalize. In verbal communication there is immediate feedback. I know by looking at a person if that person comprehends the message.

Communication is 85 percent nonverbal (this percentage varies across studies, but it is consistently within the majority). Sending a message or speaking to someone is called explicit communication, which represents only a minority of the information content in human communication. Of much greater importance is the implicit communication, such as gestures, facial expressions, information about people's environment (for example, whether their office door is open or closed), or biographical information about people in a conversation (what their job position is and what they had for lunch).

Management of relationships is critical in the open source work environment. This process includes control and coordination. Relationships between individuals and particular relationships such as management—team member relationships and relationships between team members—need to be explicitly supported and nurtured. These relationships may be affected by other factors, for example, a previous experience of working together and the number of team members. Also, the relationships between teams must be clarified and managed.

Control

Control is the process of attempting to ensure that a person or team works toward and attains certain specified organizational goals and objectives. But open source managers must shift from control of the process to facilitating the effective performance of the process. Open source managers need to change to an outcome-based measurement system. They must develop new strategies to evaluate and monitor the performance of the members' work. To work effectively in a geographically distributed environment, team members must have managerial autonomy, or the tacit permission from management to make independent decisions in the performance of their work process.

Coordination

Coordination is the process of combining the activities of different team members in order to accomplish the goals and objectives of the organization. Coordination of open source activities becomes more complex, as goals and priorities must be communicated to individuals in a variety of different locations, often with different local needs.

In a conventional office the context aids the management of work activities. Managers use face-to-face communication with subordinates, through scheduled meetings or on an informal, unscheduled basis, to communicate goals and priorities and coordinate work activities.

In the open source environment on the other hand, managers must develop new methods of coordinating a dispersed team. This is especially true in globally distributed open source teams, as team members in different countries may have dramatically different needs.

In addition, the distributed team members themselves often need new coordination mechanisms within the team to efficiently assign work activities, prevent redundant activities from occurring, and effectively perform interdependent activities in an open source environment.

Knowledge Management

Another key issue in open source is *knowledge management*. Knowledge management is the access to and creation of the tacit and explicit knowledge by the team members.

The members in an open source team potentially create a new, rich base of knowledge for the organization. Members in different locations develop different perspectives, have different experiences, and gain new knowledge from their varied work environments as they gather valuable information from customers or other organizations. As the members are scattered it becomes more difficult to manage the explicit information. It is critical and often more complex than in co-located work, to make sure that the members get access to the right information to do their job.

Tacit knowledge, or the mental models and know-how of the work process, are distributed in the project through socialization between members. This knowledge must be recognized and managed effectively; otherwise it can create problems. Significant differences in perception and understanding of individual knowledge should be recognized to enable effective performance of open source work. If these differences are not addressed, diverse cultural and political expectations may lead to unresolvable differences.

However, to improve work it is necessary to have an explicit strategy to develop and share information, as well as to help team members understand the differences and similarities among various global markets and consumer preferences.

Also, this complex environment demands development of organized knowledge acquisition and dissemination processes. It also demands structured processes to support individual and team learning.

Knowledge management is particularly critical to success in open source projects. If knowledge is poorly managed, this can be a clear source of failure; however, if it is well managed, there is great potential for increased learning and knowledge creation.

Technology Management

While technology alone will not create an effective open source environment, an effective communication technology management strategy is crucial to success. There are three communication options:

Face-to-face. Both formally and informally structured, as in the use of EDI, transaction processing, and MIS/EIS systems for managing and reporting the structured tasks.

Semi-structured. Used in version handling systems such as CVS, groupware systems, or workflow systems.

Unstructured. Used in face-to-face (when available), email, news groups, chat, and so forth.

For every business process the IT strategy should integrate the entire range of these interactions. Furthermore it is essential to have explicit management attention to this. For example, use of email and discussion forums should include social and personal interactions, and should not be restricted to purely narrow business uses.

Team members must be not only able to access computerized information and communicate electronically; they must also have the necessary skills, support, and incentives to integrate the technology into their work practices.

Open source is about collaboration, but collaboration is a trend in itself, not necessarily driven by open source. Therefore, it is worthwhile taking a look at these trends.

Technology is a key trend driver. A good indicator of IT growth is the acceptance of email. Although email is an asynchronous communication tool and works best in one-to-one communications, it is still the major tool for coordination on distributed projects today. The Internet is increasingly interactive and collaborative, and vendors are incorporating collaborative functionality into new versions of Web-based products.

Cultural change is another key driver for collaboration. The Internet gives us greater insights into other cultures. In former days we traveled thousands of miles, taking days out of our regular routines to meet with people in other countries; today, desktop video and data conferencing provide an immediate, inexpensive, and minimally disruptive method to conduct roughly the same meeting.

Implementing any new technology or program forces changes in the organization, many of which are characterized by new team structures. Teamwork behaviors create new relationships and new ways to work. Businesses must reinvent themselves and their project management methods to meet these challenges and take maximum advantage of these enabling collaborative technologies.

Collaborative behaviors are required if we are to nurture new relationships and develop new ways to work. Existing hierarchical organizational structures and processes are insufficient to meet today's demands. The increasing velocity and volume of information require an environment where right decisions can be made quickly.

Organizations change through projects more so than through regular day-to-day business operations. Massive change efforts are driven through projects and project teams.

Teamwork technologies and project management tools certainly support new ways to work by enabling a technical platform to deal with collaboration-oriented project problems. They are key components of any effort to establish enterprise project-based collaboration, and must be carefully evaluated, selected, and deployed.

However, a collaborative project environment is a *sociotechnical environment*— a community. Focusing exclusively on the technical issues provides a path to almost certain failure. The people and processes must be aligned in order to leverage the knowledge effectively.

The most important lesson to learn when working with electronic collaboration and team-oriented knowledge systems is that while the technologies and infrastructure are new, interesting, and powerful, they are only one part of the picture.

Focusing on the people issues dramatically increases the potential for success. The human factor is much more complex and cannot be underestimated in its ability to make or break collaborative improvement efforts. Technology is but a platform and a tool.

Project Management Activities

Thoughts about management have existed as long as has man. In both Greek and Roman classical literature, different ways of management and leadership are described. Many well-known works contain eternal truths and parallels to today's discussions about leadership and management.

Marcus Aurelius, Macciavelli, Moses, and King Oedipus represent some classical ways of leadership, but also four very different styles of leadership. The difference is due partly on different views on the outlook on people—mankind as good or evil, rational or irrational—partly on decision making and the demands of leadership, as well as self-knowledge of the leader.

Every situation demands its own style of leadership, but the outlook on people and self-knowledge is a general criterion. For example, Marc Aurelius had great respect for his collaborators and also had the self-knowledge to understand his strengths and weaknesses. Machiavelli's ideal was quite the contrary.

Open source project leadership is about coaching. The project manager is tasked with leading this effort, and coordinating communications, time, activities, finances, and relationships across and throughout the stakeholder audience and the domains of the enterprise. The following capabilities are required:

➣ Respect for the individual

➣ Motivation

➣ Immediate feedback

➣ Clear and explicit target orientation

Also, the following technical project management capabilities are needed: team and stakeholder communications, tracking of project specifications and changes, project planning, estimating and task definition, risk management, deliverables tracking, issues management, financial tracking and budgeting, resource scheduling, and time management.

The difficulty lies with the relationship between technology and the people who have to use it. Quantifying this reality results in Coleman's Law: *"People resist change, and organizations resist change to an exponentially greater degree."*

A corollary to this law is: *"The larger the organization, the greater the change, or the more complex the project, the greater the exponent for the resistance to change."*

Resistance to change is not unique to collaborative project management environments. It is true of any new technology or change in business process. The up side and down side of collaboration technology is that these have such a great impact on the way people work and communicate that it magnifies the degree of change, and this creates strong opinions either for or against the technology. Planning for change drastically improves the probability of success.

Motivation Encourages Project Collaboration

Because people *are* the collaboration, motivation is a monumental challenge in open source. Although many organizations aspire to establish a collaborative project management culture, collaboration is all too often just given lip service. Organizations tend to not motivate, compensate, or reward for collaboration, even though they publicly promote teamwork, communication, and cooperation. For example, how many of you reading this are compensated for how well you collaborate? How many of you have been compensated for being part of a project discussion that resulted in a good decision, a reduction in schedule, an increase in quality? What if half of your salary or some large percentage of your bonus was determined by others you interact with on a team? What if this was influenced by your customers' feedback? How would your behavior change?

However, recognition is also a reward that works better with some roles for motivation. For example, technical and R&D people, the common people in open source, respond better to peer recognition than they do to monetary rewards. Sales and marketing people on the other hand consider cash a great motivator.

The behavioral ramifications of such motivators are obvious, and we must concede that it would be more effective if organizations motivated people for the desired behaviors or outcomes.

If project managers want the team members to deliver high-quality and customer-satisfactory solutions, rewards must be based on their demand, like peer recognition, work satisfaction, and responsiveness in the team. People overwhelmingly behave as they are rewarded, and the motivational aspects of collaboration must be considered if cultural resistance is to be overcome.

Necessary Competencies

As business increasingly becomes global, organizations find themselves with open source projects that span business units, geographic regions, and organizational boundaries. Massive global expansions, cooperative partnerships, strategic alliances, frequent acquisitions and mergers—all of these drive more people to work with peers, managers, and subordinates in different locations or countries in a distributed team environment. The result is that the ability to effectively manage these types of teams through communities is critical for today's organizations to function effectively.

An electronic community is a group of people that have a common goal and interact electronically on a regular basis. They have established norms for communication and know about each other.

An open source community enables and encourages people to create a common language, to share knowledge, and to communicate, cooperate, and collaborate in both a synchronous and asynchronous, real-world manner. This can be successful only when we learn to identify and select appropriate tools that support collaboration, and when we provide people with appropriate training and defined, effective project processes.

Computer-supported collaborative work (CSCW), refers to the field of study that examines the design, adoption, and use of groupware. Despite the name, this field of study is not restricted to issues of *cooperation* or *work*, but also examines competition, socialization, and play. The field typically attracts those interested in software design and social and organizational behavior, including business people, computer scientists, organizational psychologists, communications researchers, and anthropologists, among other specialties.

In open source literature, there is much discussion on the use of information technology to support open source and virtual teams. Almost all of this discussion focuses on the uses of collaboration support tools such as email, on-line discussions and real-time chats, and other types of groupware such as workflow management systems, document management systems, and related technologies. These are important IT tools, but are not sufficient for effective management in this work environment.

Most project managers today use traditional project management software tools like Microsoft Project, whether they are managing a small project or one that has people distributed across the world. Today, there are new Web-based tools available for distributed project management, but these tools are not a "silver bullet" solution. Much more is needed to provide leadership to distributed teams and successfully facilitate projects.

Communication between people is typically highly structured. When someone asks a question, they usually expect either an answer or a request for clarification. After a request, a typical response is to fulfill the request or specify a reason for not doing so. When someone fills out a form, it usually has a predetermined route through an organization, possibly to a manager for a signature, an administrator for processing and filing, with perhaps a duplicate sent back to the original sender.

Most actions have a known range of responses and people to handle them. Communication has structure; it is interactive. The proof of successful communication is response.

When the type of structure is known, systems can take advantage of the structure to speed up communications and minimize errors. When the system determines exactly how the conversation is structured, this is known as a *technologically mediated communication structure*.

The open source way is *socially mediated communication*. When someone wants to make a request, they send, for instance, a plain email message to another person, and that person decides whether to respond, how to respond, and who to respond to.

Socially mediated communication can be more time-consuming and prone to error, and thus it may be unacceptable for certain types of organizations, especially ones that allow no exceptions to protocol, such as the military or certain safety-critical organizations. On the other hand, exceptions to the expected structure of communication are extremely common. It is rather a rule than an exception that information really takes the officially directed route. Informal structures built on trust and respect (different from the official structure) exist in every organization.

Thus, technologically mediated communication may actually be an obstruction to getting work done efficiently and may lead people to not use a groupware system or obstruct it. Technologically mediated communication is usually technologically enforced communication.

We are still quite far from developing the grand groupware system that encompasses every type of communication, and we will probably never get there. The possibilities are constantly evolving with changes in both our patterns of social interaction and the available technology.

To be effective in an open source environment, managers need to reflect deeply and act effectively. They need to draw on theory and experience, manage an evolving understanding of the situation, and develop insights that frame effective action.

These technologies provide a base for open source work, but not a solution. Communication and collaboration will become activities integrated with, and natural components of, all aspects of daily, electronically mediated work. Groupware of all types will move into the infrastructure, providing powerful and widely used technologies. This provides a context—electronically mediated work environments—in which the thrust of the information architecture of the enterprise can become something substantially different from that of the past: enhancing personal power to think and act more effectively.

This is particularly important in open source projects. Simply supporting communication and collaboration with these basic technologies is not by itself sufficient. Effective management of open source requires much more than basic communication and collaboration technologies. What is needed is an IT architecture that supports participants in a open source work organization by providing the tools and techniques to manage the subtle issues of open source work, in a pragmatic and focussed way.

In an open source project, managers have to manage effectively in a world rich with information, which is continuously changing. The ways in which a manager manages the personal information can be critical to that person's effectiveness. This is especially true in an open source environment where people do not have day-to-day, face-to-face contact with all of their work-related partners, and the complexity of information to be absorbed and used is even greater than in a stable, single-location work environment. For example, a global team with participants in 5 or 20 countries must keep track of official work holidays in each of the countries.

To deal with this complexity, people need help in managing large quantities of personal and shared soft information. This information is evolving dynamically and needs to be updated. Because it includes large quantities of small bits of personal information, it is complex. Thus, the members need ways of constructing views of the information, which display filtered and sorted subsets of the information in meaningful ways. Such views can help the individual to gain new insights and perspectives, and to identify and focus on key issues and potential actions to take. The simple juxtaposition of different notes taken at different times can stimulate insights. Printing out some views can be useful, such as printing out a to-do list or a list of all of the issues that need to be discussed with a specific team member.

Groupware

Managing an open source team requires computer-aided tools called *groupware*. As organizations realize the value of capturing and accessing both strategic and tactical collaboration for future reference, the ability of groupware to support and log real-time and asynchronous collaboration to support knowledge management initiatives has grown. This affects the need for system reliability on two levels:

Robust support for real-time and project collaboration. System uptime and performance speed become even more important when they are used for real-time collaboration and short-term tactical collaboration projects.

Search capacity. Lost files and inaccessibility limit the ability of organizations to capitalize on their electronic collaborative knowledge assets.

Groupware is technology designed to facilitate the work of groups. This technology is used to communicate between group members, coordinate work, and so forth. While traditional technologies like the telephone technically qualify as groupware, the term groupware refers to email, newsgroups, videophones, or chat.

Groupware technologies are typically divided in four groups: whether members of the group are working together at the same time or at different times, and whether users are working together in the same place or in different places. (See Table 7.2.)

In videoconferencing, simply providing a wide-angle camera lens can provide a greater degree of environmental awareness. In email, smileys, simple information about the time and date of the message, or the signature file of the sender (that is, with contact info, company info, and so on) gives context for making sense of the message.

Obviously, awareness can be at odds with privacy concerns, and as the previous section indicated, it's important to give users control over how much information about themselves is made available to others.

Table 7.2   Groupware Technology Groups

	SAME TIME, SYNCHRONOUS OR REAL TIME	DIFFERENT TIME, ASYNCHRONOUS
Same Place, "Face-to-Face"	Voting, presentation support	Shared computers
Different Place, "Distance"	Videoconferencing, chat, ICQ	Email, workflow, revision handling systems

This is not entirely a technical design issue, but is an issue we must be aware of as a community—we will often want increasingly more information from others, and the social and economic pressure to share this information will increase over time. As a society, we are obligated to be sensitive to when we are asking for too much information and find other ways of achieving our common objectives without compromising individual privacy.

In-house projects make easier the use of more advanced groupware technologies, as a company can standardize on advanced technology such as video-conferencing.

It is important to understand how groups behave and how people behave in groups. It is also important to have a good understanding of networking technology and how aspects of that technology, for instance, delays in synchronizing views, affect a user's experience.

Many aspects of groups require special consideration. Large groups behave differently from small groups, but the performance parameters of the technologies to support different groups vary.

Groupware must be easier to use than single-user systems, as the pace of a conversation often drives the pace of use of an application. Responsiveness and reliability are significant issues.

It is important to understand the degree of homogeneity of the members, of the possible roles different people play in cooperative work, and of who are the decision makers and what influences them.

Asynchronous Groupware

Email is by far the most common groupware application (besides, of course, the traditional telephone). While the basic technology is designed to pass simple messages between two people, even relatively basic email systems typically include features for automatically filtering and forwarding messages, filing messages, creating mailing groups, and attaching files with a message. Other features that have been explored include automatic sorting and processing of messages, automatic routing, and structured communication (that is, messages requiring certain information).

Newsgroups and mailing lists are similar to email systems except that they are intended for messages among large groups of people instead of one-to-one communication. In practice the main difference between newsgroups and mailing lists is that newsgroups only show messages to a user when they are explicitly requested (an *on-demand service*), while mailing lists deliver messages as they become available (an *interrupt-driven* interface).

A revision control system, such as the Concurrent Versions System (CVS), allows team members (or anyone, actually) immediate access to the latest version of the project's source code; it facilitates the creation of patch files necessary for contributing bug fixes and new features on a software project, and it allows active developers to hack away at the same code base.

Workflow systems allow documents to be routed throughout organizations via a relatively fixed process. A simple example of a workflow application is an expense report: An employee enters and submits an expense report; a copy is archived then routed to the employee's manager for approval; the manager receives the document, electronically approves it, and sends it on; and the expense is registered to the group's account and forwarded to the accounting department for payment. Workflow systems may provide features such as routing, development of forms, and support for differing roles and privileges.

Group calendars allow scheduling, project management, and coordination among many members. Typical features detect when schedules conflict or find meeting times that will work for everyone. Group calendars also help to locate people. Typical concerns are privacy (users may feel that certain activities are not public matters), and completeness and accuracy (users may feel that the time it takes to enter schedule information is not justified by the benefits of the calendar).

Collaborative writing systems may provide both real-time support and non-real-time support. Word processors may provide asynchronous support by showing authorship and by allowing users to track changes and make annotations to documents.

Authors collaborating on a document may also be given tools to help plan and coordinate the authoring process, such as methods for locking parts of the document or linking separately authored documents. Synchronous support allows authors to see each other's changes as they make them, and usually needs to provide an additional communication channel to the authors as they work via, for example, videophones or chat.

Synchronous or Realtime Groupware

Chat and conference calls are the basic real-time groupware systems. Chat systems permit many people to write messages in real time in a public space. As each person submits a message, it appears at the bottom of a scrolling screen.

While chat-like systems are possible using nontext media, the text version of chat has the rather interesting aspect of having a direct transcript of the conversation, which not only has long-term value, but also allows for backward reference during conversation. This makes it easier for people to drop into a conversation and still pick up on the ongoing discussion.

Shared whiteboards allow two or more people to view and draw on a shared drawing surface even from different locations. This can be used, for instance, during a phone call, where each person can take notes or work collaboratively on a visual problem.

Most shared whiteboards are designed for informal conversation, but they may also serve structured communications or more sophisticated drawing tasks, such as collaborative graphic design, publishing, or engineering applications.

Shared whiteboards can indicate where each person is drawing or pointing by showing telepointers that are color-coded or labeled to identify each person.

Videocommunications systems allow several people to talk to and see each other. It is essentially a telephone system with an additional video camera.

Cost and compatibility issues limited early use of video systems to scheduled videoconference meeting rooms. Video is advantageous when visual information is being discussed, but may not provide substantial benefit in most cases where conventional audio telephones are adequate. In addition to supporting conversations, video may also be used in less direct collaborative situations, such as by providing a view of activities at a remote location.

Decision Support Systems

Decision support systems are designed to facilitate groups in decision making. They provide tools for brainstorming, examining ideas, putting weights and probabilities on events and alternatives, and voting. Such systems enable presumably more rational and even-handed decisions. Primarily designed to facilitate meetings, they encourage equal participation by, for example, providing anonymity or enforcing taking turns.

To complicate matters, there is another group of project management related tools called project management support tools (to differentiate them from tools that focus on managing resources and tasks). These tools present themselves either as add-ons to existing project management tools, such as for MS Project, or as stand-alone tools that focus on one or a few specific project-related issues.

Such tools seek to address risk management, cost estimation, and vendor management, for example. In closing, it is important to offer a caveat. Project management tools are not project management. Tools are no substitute for effective project management methodologies and communications practices.

Nor will they act as a substitute for an effective culture that can support and enable people to take high-level responsibility for their own contributions to the projects they are assigned.

Tools must be seen for what they are: enablers for the effective management of information and knowledge related to the project process and environment. Project managers who attempt to rely on the tools to *do* the management of the project will inevitably fail, as will their projects.

People make progress; the tools are just enablers. In our practice, we find that with the implementation of these new and more *social* tools, interpersonal interactions must be considered and are responsible for failures about 80 percent of the time. A holistic approach to taking on any collaborative projects definitely will increase the chances of success.

Teamware is a specialized kind of groupware or an extension to groupware that provides a shared, virtual space that actively supports team members in defining shared goals, provides the means to achieve those goals, and provides a way to track progress toward those goals.

Teamware software combines various categories from the previous groupware as a team framework, including workflow, document handling, instant messaging, and in some cases, electronic whiteboarding and brainstorming toolsets.

The Groupware Configuration Process

When implementing a groupware tool for an open source team, it is important to have a solid understanding of the members, what their goals are, and how they go about their work. For broadly targeted groupware applications, such as videoconferencing or email lists, understanding members boils down to understanding how human beings communicate in the first place, keeping in mind that:

➤ Organizing and scheduling for groups is more difficult than for individuals.

➤ Group interaction style is hard to select for beforehand, whereas individual characteristics are often possible to determine before a study is conducted.

➤ Preestablished groups vary in interaction style, and the length of time they've been a group affects their communication patterns.

➤ New groups change quickly during the group formation process.

➤ Groups are dynamic; roles change.

➤ Many studies need to be long term, especially when studying asynchronous groupware.

➣ Modifying prototypes can be technically difficult because of the added complexity of groupware over single-user software.

➣ In software for large organizations, testing new prototypes can be difficult or impossible because of the disruption caused by introducing new versions into an organization.

Groupware systems cannot be successful unless a critical mass of users chooses to use the system. Two of the most common reasons for failing to achieve critical mass are lack of interoperability and the lack of appropriate individual benefit.

For example, in the early 1990s, AT&T and MCI both introduced videophones commercially, but as there were no standards the two systems couldn't communicate with each other. The systems had no "network effect." This lack of interoperability and compatibility meant that anyone who wanted to buy a videophone had to make sure that everyone they wanted to talk to would buy the same system. Compatibility issues lead to general wariness among customers, who want to wait until a clear standard has emerged.

Today there are standards for videoconferencing, and cheap Web cameras are replacing the expensive videophones. But the technology still needs high-speed networks, at least 128 kbps ISDN.

I believe that, ultimately, people will want to be able to collaborate in real time using any of these mediums. Currently, video is expensive, difficult, and requires additional hardware and significant bandwidth. We see this changing rapidly. Some vendors are doing hybrid solutions between data- and videoconferencing (for example, broadcast video over NetMeeting, with interactive dataconferencing).

Choosing the Right Product

When choosing the right groupware product, flexibility and functionality should be considered only in relation to reliability and performance.

Explore and evaluate the following areas to gain insight into product reliability, performance, and cost of administration:

Customer references. The real test of user satisfaction and reliability is not in test labs, but with actual users. Vendors should be willing to supply customer references that can tell a prospective purchaser how many users per server, users per administrator, minutes of unplanned downtime, and other administrative issues they have experienced with the product.

Long-standing customers. Beyond standard reference sites, long-standing customers who have gone beyond the honeymoon can share valuable insight about the pleasure—and pain—of sticking with an application. While six years may be extreme for many new products, vendors should be able to produce references with a rollout date near the product launch date.

Product development team. Both age and evolution of a product affects its reliability and performance. Key to a reliable product is the caliber of engineers writing functional and technical specifications and how they communicate with one another. A focused development team is more likely to produce a reliable product in the long term than a disjointed or distributed one—or one that built numerous versions of the product with co-op student help over a number of years.

Underlying infrastructure. Reliable, high-performance products manage the balance between a highly flexible component architecture and a monolithic one. Where there are many components, the product will have numerous potential points of failure. Where it is monolithic, it can be too rigid to change with the needs of the organization. The ideal solution has a core level that manages the basic necessary functions, an application layer, and one layer of self-contained devices that function independently of each other and communicate with each, if at all, through the core application.

Prior release schedule. Were previous releases of the product major fixes, or minor adjustments? The greater the number of major fixes, the greater the possibility that there are conflicting or inefficient functional specifications built into the product that will affect reliability and performance.

Company vision. What is the company saying about what it provides? Has that message been consistent over the past few years, or has it been often realigned to take on the latest buzzwords? Potential customers should be wary of companies that change their marketing vision on a tactical basis—they are probably also making rapid tactical changes in products that can detract from reliability and performance.

Properties

The following are three properties to look for in a groupware program:

➢ Functionality that allows it to be extended and adapted to a wide variety of tasks and situations, including unanticipated ones

➢ Support for standards, which enable it to be deployed on a wide variety of platforms

➢ Features that contribute to a shared social identity and trust

It is all about the social and community aspects of the collaboration environment. A usable groupware must support and encourage desirable behavior. However, project management also requires additional tools with specific project enabling functionality.

While groupware usually only provides an infrastructure for communications and collaboration around generic information, specific project management capabilities are required. Project management tools provide support for the fundamental project activities of project initiation and planning, and the ongoing tasks of project control and reporting. Project control activities include the tracking of progress, reporting of effort to date, and current financial variance from the initial baseline.

The lines between groupware and project management software are beginning to blur as organizations demand project and team collaboration. Many project management tool vendors and groupware vendors are porting their software to the Internet. They are, respectively, incorporating collaboration capabilities with project management features.

Project management software today ranges from using the Internet as a way to simply share project information, to innovative redesign of groupware with project environments that support a collaborative work team or an electronic project community space.

To effectively manage distributed projects and teams, both the collaborative software capabilities of groupware and specific project management features are required.

Obtaining a Critical Mass

Even when everyone in the group may benefit, if individuals make the choice, the system may not succeed. Examples are calendar systems like Microsoft Exchange or Centrinity First Class, Web-based calendars like My Yahoo!, or off-line group calendars like Symantec Act! If everyone enters all of their appointments, then everyone has the benefit of being able to safely schedule around other people's appointments.

However, if it's not easy to enter your appointments, then it may be perceived by users as more beneficial to leave their own appointments off, while viewing other people's appointments. The application must be perceived as useful for individuals even outside the context of full group adoption.

First, in a situation where the cooperating actors have limited information-processing capacities, it is important to prevent potential inefficiencies by avoiding information overflows.

Second, the increased potential for control and monitoring impacts the right to informational self-determination and privacy. Thus, the dual ambivalence of transparency, namely control and processing capacity, requires a balance when constructing shared information spaces by implementing selective transparency using filtering and authentication mechanisms.

This disparity of individual and group benefit is discussed in game theory as the *prisoner's dilemma* or *the commons problem*. It is exactly the same problem as with public domain discussed in Chapter 3, "The Open Source Philosophy": responsibility.

If a village has a common land for grazing cattle, then this area can be a strong benefit to the community as long as everyone uses it with restraint. If no one takes responsibility (or claims the ownership, which is another side of the same coin), the grass will be consumed and the cows will be without food, and the whole village is worse off as a result.

Open source is a common land, in the way that it is built on voluntariness. Individuals have the incentive to "graze as many cattle as possible on the commons" as opposed to their own private property. Misused, the asset, in this case trust and respect, will be destroyed. Most people are familiar with the problem of spamming with email. Some other common violations of social protocol include taking inappropriate advantage of anonymity, sabotaging group work, or violating privacy.

To solve this problem, groups can apply social pressure to enforce groupware use, as in having the boss insist that it's used. The open source, straightforward solution is to regulate and moderate.

In managing open source projects, information needs to be shared. The more information that gets shared, the more easily common ground can be achieved. Sharing information about yourself enables many systems to provide more useful customization and matching to your interests.

While anonymity can protect an individual, there are also quite legitimate reasons for identifying people for accountability, especially where security and the risk of abusive behavior are involved.

To resolve these conflicting needs, it's important to give open source members as much control as possible over what information gets shared and what remains private. Let members decide how much information to share, and use that to determine what kinds of information they can access. One example of privacy policy is the principle of reciprocity: If a user wants information about another user, then they must provide the equivalent information about themselves. Reciprocity isn't always the right policy, but it does serve as a useful starting point.

When groups are working in real time with the same information, they may need customized views of the information. The challenge of customized views is to support the establishment of a common ground, or shared understanding of what information is known and shared between the different users.

It is important to make it very clear what information is private and what is shared, and as much as possible make it clear what information the other user is seeing, for instance, provide a miniature or summary view of the other person's screen.

In all cases, be sure to maintain consistency of the data. Users should never see spurious or irreconcilable differences.

Rules and protocols for electronic meetings are very important. The moderator needs to take control over two issues: the session and the floor, that is, decide who is allowed to join the discussion and what is allowed in the discussion.

A session is a situation in which a group of people is in a conversation at a given time. Session control is like a person standing at the door of a room checking IDs and deciding who gets to enter. Floor control involves what you get to do once you're inside the room.

Session control issues include finding out what rooms are available, determining who can enter and exit the room, and when and how. The basic policies for session control are:

➤ Decide what limits there are to who can join a session. Are there limits to the number of people or to who is qualified to enter?

➤ Allow people to join and leave at any time. Provide a "polite" protocol for doing so. Let people comfortably enter and leave conversations through continuous degrees of commitment and intrusion.

➤ Avoid intrusive situations where users are able to invade privacy or impose a session on others. A telephone call is an example of an intrusive session control mechanism. In the absence of an answering machine or caller ID, a person has no way of determining whether a call is desired or not.

➤ Provide a means for preventing interruptions.

➤ Facilitate people getting together. Provide mechanisms for identifying appropriate conversational partners.

➤ Provide a means for setting up side conferences.

Once people have joined a discussion, it must be decided what kind of access each person has to shared conversational properties. A member can be a listener who participates in the discussion or a moderator who controls the discussion.

Simultaneous access by everyone to everything is often preferred for the most fluid conversation, but it can be vulnerable, especially with a large number of people, to just a single non-cooperative person. The advantages to providing some kind of mediated access include preventing mistakes, preventing unauthorized access, and avoiding people making conflicting changes. There can also be multiple whiteboards. Some may be personal and others shared. Personal whiteboards may be visible to some users but noneditable by other users. This allows everyone to work simultaneously without interfering with the work of others.

Interfaces and Documentation

There are two important parameters that describe a successful distributed open source project: *interfaces* and *documentation*. Documentation is just as important as the design itself to capture the process leading to a design. This may sound trivial, but it is especially true for an open source project in which the team members have no history of prior collaboration and cannot readily foresee conflicts or bottlenecks in the design process. Note the following points about documentation:

> ➤ Internet-based design documentation is immediately accessible to all participants, whether working asynchronously or while reviewing the information during a conference call.

> ➤ The documentation is decentralized, allowing groups to maintain ownership and editorial control of their contributions.

> ➤ The Web allows searching according to different interests (for example, project administration, optical systems, controls). With the continued development of better searching tools, we expect this capability to become increasingly important.

> ➤ Access to shared, comprehensive online documentation accelerates the process of reaching consensus.

Internet-based documentation is useful for bringing new team members up to speed during the design and redesign projects, by looking at these Web pages and sending a note to the team manager when they have digested the material.

A second use of the Web is for learning about and revisiting tools and services used during a project. When revisiting an infrequently used tool, engineers often prefer to go back to their notebooks to review how they used the tool on previous occasions, rather than diving straight into the generic documentation provided by the tool's creators. A working design example should help to understand how the tools work, what they are good for, when they fail, and why. It is likely that the tool was previously used in a context similar to the present one, and the extra contextual information, as well as any applications tips that were recorded in the earlier case, help the team members to get reacquainted.

Open source differs from a conventional industrial project in that it is a community effort with no formal top-down management structure and no central authority. Extensive discussion is needed to determine responsibility and aspects of the design. An open source Web site usually becomes a large and complex set of interconnected project webs.

The online documentation contains a mix of formal information (the code or the content) and informal information in the form of electronic mail messages, and so forth.

Human Interaction

Despite the commitment of open source team members to exploit the Internet for collaboration, a considerable amount of travel and face-to-face contact is needed. The main reason is that it is essential for team members to assimilate the local culture as well as the organizational structure of other teams to cooperate effectively.

One does not easily learn, for example, that a particular technician at another site is shy and does not speak up during group videoconferences or respond to broadcast solicitations for feedback by email, but is very competent and should be consulted directly.

An interesting question is whether the sophistication of online open source interaction environments like MOOs and MUDs will evolve to the point that these essential human elements can be assimilated electronically.

Advances in session creation and management are also needed, along with better procedures for capturing and reusing session information. To be used regularly, online videoconferencing tools must become as convenient as the competition: telephones, faxes, and email.

Summary

Open source as an application development method is basically managing a bunch of scattered volunteer developers in a single project. To be practically manageable, the team needs some kind of organization and management.

When people are separated geographically from each other, they must work more autonomously and be prepared to make decisions independently.

Working in an open source team is a very different experience from working face-to-face. The principal issues are the lack of face-to-face contact, difficulties of disambiguating communication, feelings of isolation, and difficulties in trusting other team members.

Open source project leadership is about coaching. The project manager is tasked with leading this effort, and coordinating communications, time, activities, finances, and relationships across and throughout the stakeholder audience and the domains of the enterprise.

Managing an open source team requires groupware and decision support systems, which will be covered in the next chapter.

CHAPTER 8

Tools for Building Open Source Products

When the only tool you own is a hammer,
every problem begins to resemble a nail.

ABRAHAM H. MASLOW, *MASLOW ON MANAGEMENT*,
JOHN WILEY & SONS INC., 1998

As open source today is more or less used only in programming projects, all available tools are made for software development activities. But one should not forget that the open source technique is general and can be used for any project.

There are two kinds of open software tools: the tools for building products and the tools for managing a project. The following types of tools are needed to build an open source product:

PRODUCT MANAGEMENT TOOLS

A version handling system

A problem management tool

PROJECT MANAGEMENT TOOLS

A clearinghouse for open source projects (discussed in Chapter 10, "Setting Up an Open Source Project")

A groupware system (optional; discussed in Chapter 7, "Managing Distributed Open Source Projects")

There are many commercial software development tools, but as this is a book on open source, we will only cover open source development tools. There are a few freely available problem management tools. Generally you must transfer them from an archive site on the Internet using FTP or HTTP. In some cases, the tool must be compiled at the local site, and in some cases there is a license fee. Most come bundled with adequate documentation. Such tools generally are provided without support.

Version Handling Systems

Version handling systems help multiple users make simultaneous changes to a collection of documents and files, without clobbering each other's work or resulting in version confusion.

Version control is essential for software development and is often used for managing Web sites, documentation, engineering drawings, corporate legal and business documents, and other documentation that must be archived and controlled. Version control also blends into specialties of related interest.

Document Control and Image Retrieval

Document control systems tend to focus more on the management of a large collection of documents and/or images, rather than on maintaining differing versions of a smaller number of documents.

Configuration Management and Software Distribution

Version control tools are often used to store and control the configuration files (for example, AUTOEXEC.BAT or /etc/resolv.conf) for an operating system or software package. Administrators of large corporate networks turn to configuration management tools to guard against the accidental corruption of a config file, and to guarantee a uniform system configuration for a collection of workstations and servers. Configuration management tools are often integrated with software distribution tools, which automate the deployment and update of software packages across a large number of desktops.

Software Metrics

When engineering or programming staff are making many changes during product development, management is often interested in statistics about the rate of change. Files that change a lot and repeatedly over long periods of time often indicate trouble spots. Software metrics are tools that can help locate trouble spots by generating statistics about code and changes in that code.

Bug-Tracking and Problem Reports

Because software change is often driven by problem reports, it is natural to integrate bug-tracking tools with version control systems. This allows for a framework where changes resulting from a bug report can be easily located, and where some measure of certainty is provided that all changes have been integrated into a product release. This may not be an issue for small projects, but for anything much larger, say a half dozen or more developers, a few dozen released patches, and more than a few actively supported releases, such integration is mandatory.

Concurrent Versions System

By far the most popular version handling system used is the *Concurrent Versions System* (CVS) (www.cvshome.org). It has a broad use and is useful for everyone from individual developers to large distributed teams. Its client-server access method lets developers access the latest code from any Internet connection. Its unreserved check-out model of version control avoids artificial conflicts common with the exclusive check-out model. And its client tools are available on most platforms.

CVS is a configuration management system that records the history of source code files. Version control systems are valuable for anyone, but software development teams usually use them. Developers working on a team need to be able to coordinate their individual changes. A central version control system allows that.

When the software is modified, bugs often occur but are usually not detected until a while after the modification is made. With CVS, you can easily retrieve old versions to see exactly which change caused the bug. A version control system keeps a history of the changes made to a set of files. For a developer, that means being able to keep track of all the changes made to a program during the entire development time. Instead of manually saving every version of every file ever created, CVS stores only the differences between versions, pretty much like a backup system, which saves a lot of disk space.

CVS also takes care of different people working on the same file in the project. It is all too easy to overwrite each other's changes. Some editors, like GNU Emacs, try to make sure that two people never modify the same file at the same time, but this conflict-avoiding scheme only works if all are using

GNU Emacs. If someone is using another editor the protection will not work. CVS solves this problem by isolating the different developers' works in separate directories. CVS then merges the work when each developer is done.

It is possible to run CVS on a local machine. Development teams, however, need a central server that all members can access to serve as the repository for their code. CVS has built-in client-server access methods so that any developer who can connect to the Internet can access files on a CVS server.

In traditional version control systems, a developer checks out a file, modifies it, then checks in the file. The developer who checks out a file has exclusive rights to modify it, and no one else can check out the file. Only the developer who checked out the file can check in modifications.

In a large open source project, with developers all over the world working in any time zone, it is not practical to give one developer the ability to prevent every other developer from working on a file. The only practical way to get work done is to be able to work on a project whenever one wants to. CVS solves this problem with its *unreserved check-out model*: Checking out a file doesn't give a developer exclusive rights to that file. Other developers can also check it out, make their own modifications, and check it back in. CVS detects when multiple developers make changes to the same file and automatically merges those changes, but only as long as the changes are not made to the same lines of code. If CVS can't safely resolve the changes, the developer will have to merge them manually.

CVS is used by popular open source projects like:

Mozilla	www.mozilla.org/cvs.html
The Gimp	www.gimp.org/devel_cvs.html
Xemacs	http://cvs.xemacs.org
KDE	www.kde.org/anoncvs.html
Gnome	http://developer.gnome.org/tools/cvs.html

CVS is available in a variety of ways, including free download from the Internet. The first step is to get CVS at www.cvshome.org/dev/codes.html.

Installing CVS is usually just a matter of unpacking it from the archive you downloaded. Configuring CVS can be a bit tricky and is highly dependent on your platform and where your CVS code repository is stored. CVShome.org hosts "The Cederqvist" manual, the CVS manual written and edited by Per Cederqvist, a comprehensive source of CVS information (www.cvshome.org/

docs/manual/index.html). There are also a number of CVS add-ons for various platforms that add functionality to CVS and make it easier to use.

The mailing list, known as info-cvs, is devoted to CVS issues. To subscribe, send an email to info-cvs-request@gnu.org. The right usenet group for CVS discussions is comp.software.config-mgmt.

What CVS Is Not

It's easy to forget that technology is only a catalyst and not the solution. CVS is an essential tool for managing open source projects, but merely saying that you are using CVS is not a guarantee for success.

Not a Substitute for Management

As stated in previous chapters, managers and project leaders are expected to communicate to the developers. CVS does not handle schedules, merge points, branch names, and release dates.

Not a Substitute for Communication

CVS can only handle textual conflicts, arising when two changes to the same base file are near enough to trouble the merge (that is, diff3) command. It cannot determine when simultaneous changes within a single file or across a whole collection of files will logically conflict with one another. CVS cannot figure out nontextual or distributed conflicts in program logic. For example: If you change the arguments to function X defined in file A, CVS cannot detect if someone edits file B, adding new calls to function X using the old arguments.

Not a Build System

CVS does not specify how to build anything. It merely stores files for retrieval in a specified tree structure.

It does not specify how to use disk space in the checked-out working directories. Too many makefiles or scripts in the directories could make it necessary to check-out the entire repository, as they require the knowledge of the relative positions of everything else. It is possible to arrange the disk usage arbitrarily, if the work is modularized and constructed with a build system that will share files via links, mounts, VPATH in makefiles, and so on. However, this must be made and maintained manually. CVS does not specifically address these issues, but the tools created to support such a build system (scripts, makefiles, and so on) could be placed under CVS.

CVS does not figure out what files need to be rebuilt when something is changed. The best approach is to use make for building, and use some automated tool for generating the dependencies, which make uses.

Not a Change Control

CVS is not a bug-tracking tool. It can be interfaced to an external bug-tracking system like Bugzilla (see the *rcsinfo* and *verifymsg* files).

CVS cannot track changes to several files changed together as one logical change. If you check in several files in a single CVS commit operation, CVS then forgets that those files were checked in together, and the fact that they have the same log message is the only thing tying them together.

CVS cannot keep track of the status of each change, for example, if some changes have been written by one programmer and others reviewed by a second programmer.

Not a Built-in Process Model

CVS has no support for approvals. It is possible, but it must be manually handled. Features such as branches and tags can be used to perform tasks such as doing work in a development tree and then merging certain changes over to a stable tree only once they have been proven. The commands *commitinfo*, *loginfo*, *rcsinfo*, or *verifymsg* can be used to require that certain steps be performed before CVS will allow a check-in.

Aegis

Aegis is a transaction-based software configuration management system, or, more simply, a source-code control system.

PRCS

The *Project Revision Control System* (PRCS), is the front end to a set of tools that (like CVS) provides a way to deal with sets of files and directories as an entity, preserving coherent versions of the entire set. It is claimed to be easier to use than CVS, with higher performance too. PRCS currently lacks network features, although these are being developed.

RCS

The *Revision Control System* (RCS) is an industry standard collection of tools providing basic file locking and version control mechanisms. Its strength and durability are indicated by the fact that almost all other version control tools use RCS as their low-level interface—RCS is the workhorse engine. RCS is low level. It's not client-server. It's available on all Linux distributions.

SCCS

An oldie but a goodie, *Source Code Control System* (SCCS) is considered by many to be obsolete, but still has many active fans, and is in active development, in the form of GNU CSSC. Standards fans take note: the SCCS command line is standardized in the Single Unix Specification, Version 2.

Problem Reporting Tools

One of the most important advantages of using open source is that bug tracking is made much more efficient. It is important, however, to have a high-quality bug-tracking tool to support the problem finding.

Bluetail Ticket Tracker

Bluetail Ticket Tracker (BTT) (www.bluetail.com/~tobbe/btt) is a basic trouble-ticketing system. It is written in Erlang, and thus runs on Windows as well as Linux.

Bugzilla

Bugzilla (www.mozilla.org/bugs) is the problem management tool used by the Netscape Mozilla team mozilla.org. It is a database for bugs that lets programmers report bugs and assigns these to the appropriate developers. Developers can use Bugzilla to keep a to-do list as well as to prioritize, schedule, and track dependencies. The system also consists of an HTML front end to perform queries into the database.

Bugzilla's first installation was at mozilla.org but since then several companies, private and public, open source and commercial are using it to track software defects.

It is written in Perl and uses MySQL as its database back end. The source code to the Bugzilla tool itself is available. You can check it out from the Mozilla CVS server by doing:

```
cvs checkout mozilla/webtools/bugzilla
```

Documentation for Bugzilla is unfortunately spotty and spread out at best. When a bug is first reported it is assigned to the default owner of the bug's component and Bugzilla emails them with the bug report. At this time the developer will probably look at the bug and either accept it or give it to someone else. If the bug remains new and inactive for more than a week, Bugzilla sends an email a week to the bug's owner until action is taken. Whenever a bug is reassigned or has its component changed, its status is set to NEW. The NEW status means that the bug is newly added to a particular developer's plate, not that the bug is newly reported.

Debian Bug Tracking System

The Debian Bug Tracking System (www.chiark.greenend.org.uk/~ian/debbugs) is a set of scripts that maintains a database of problem reports. Key features include complete input and manipulation of bugs by email. Various lists of bugs are available via email or the Web. The system runs on Unix and expects to have its own (possibly "virtual") mail domain.

Double Choco Latte

Double Choco Latte (http://dcl.sourceforge.net) is a basic Web-based trouble-ticketing system. Implemented in PHP, with PostgresSQL or MySQL back ends. It provides basic job estimation and time-tracking, and a statistics page. Double Choco Latte requires Javascript-enabled browsers.

Frontdesk

A mail-based sorting and bug reporting system, Frontdesk (http://admin.gnacademy.org:8001/uu-gna/tech/dbedit/frontdesk.html) is a set of scripts that puts incoming mail into threaded queues, which can be accessed via the Web.

GNU GNATS

The GNU Problem Report Management System (GNU GNATS) is copyrighted by the Free Software Foundation, but freely available under the GNU General Public License. Commercial support for GNATS (under the name PRMS) is provided by Cygnus Solutions (www.cygnus.com).

The GNU GNATS has been the cornerstone of open source bug-tracking systems. The core is command-line, e-mail based, allowing additional tools and GUI wrappers to be created for it. These include wwwgnats, a Web interface, and TkGnats, a Tk interface.

This product, which helps track software problems or change requests, handles problems submitted via email and uses a file-system-based database. It can maintain an audit trail of all activities concerning a specific problem.

GNATS can be obtained from one of the GNU mirrors or from Cygnus Support. For example, GNATS may be found via anonymous FTP at ftp://prep

.ai.mit.edu/pub/gnu/gnats/ or ftp://sourceware.cygnus.com/pub/gnats. A Web interface to GNATS, gnatsweb, is distributed with GNATS itself.

HelpDesk

HelpDesk (www.jrobst.freeserve.co.uk/helpdesk.html) is a Web-based trouble-ticketing system written in Apache/modperl, with MySQL as the back end. HelpDesk is GPL'ed. Currently, HelpDesk supports only the most basic functions.

JitterBug

JitterBug (http://samba.anu.edu.au/jitterbug), is a simple Web-based bug-tracking system developed by the Samba Team to handle the huge volume of mail they get at the samba-bugs mail alias. Now used on other projects, it is Web based and written in C. Messages enter the system via email or a Web interface.

To run JitterBug you need some kind of Unix-like operating system. Ports to others should be quite easy, but haven't been done yet. You also need the ability to configure the Web daemon and chmod +s one file. Root administrator authority is only needed to install the system. It is possible to run JitterBug without this, but it is less secure. This system has been used since October 1997 with very good results.

Job Control System

Job Control System (JCS) is a free bug-reporting package (http://members .xoom.com/_XOOM/prozach/jcs.html). JCS is done up with Bourne-shell CGI scripts working from a flat-file database.

Keystone

Keystone (www.stonekeep.com) is a Web-based project and problem management system which uses a SQL server back end. It is free for up to 10 concurrent users, after which there is a small fee requested.

OpenTicket

OpenTicket (http://openticket.point-one.net) is a simple, open-source trouble-ticketing system with a SQL back end, based on Zope. A very basic system, it allows users to create tickets with various priorities and assign them to a team. OpenTicket includes a simple ticket search interface. Problem types and status are fully configurable. There is no security mechanism.

Open Track

The Open Track (www.ede.com/ot/index.html) defect and enhancement tracking system was originally distributed by Open Software Foundation (OSF), and is now maintained as an open source project by EDE. It began as a Unix-based tracking system used to manage defect reports and enhancement requests filed against offerings, tools, or projects. There is also a Windows NT port available that uses the Sleepycat Web-based database.

Defects and change requests are stored in a flat-file system. Each report is stored as a Change Request (CR) in a plain file containing project-chosen fields that describe the defect or enhancement. It does not appear to nurture any sort of user community. Source is available but oddly packaged, and there is no license to indicate how potential contributors should think of this project. Each project established in Open Track is configurable through definitions files and TCL procedures.

PHP HelpDesk

PHP HelpDesk (http://phphelpdesk.sourceforge.net) is a project to create a PHP-based bug-tracking system. It hooks up to a MySQL back end, and currently supports only the most basic functions such as ticket creation, viewing, and search.

ProManager

ProManager (http://sourceforge.net/projects/promanager) is a task-tracking tool. It uses a PHP front end and a MySQL back end. ProManager is under public-domain license.

RT

RT (www.fsck.com/projects/rt) is a Web-based bug-tracking system. Reports can be opened by email, Web, or command line. RT is written in Perl; it uses a MySQL back end. It is similar to Req and RUST in that email is a fundamental part of the system. RT includes several mailing lists and list archives.

ReqNG

ReqNG (http://reqng.sycore.reqng) is an email-based trouble-ticketing system written in Perl, with a flat-file back end system. There are many adjunct developments that include a WWWReq (www.cs.ucr.edu/~cvarner/wwwreq/), a Web-based interface; TkReq (www.cs.wisc.edu/~jmelski/tkreq/), a tcl/tk client front end; and xreq (http://teak.wiscnet.net/xreqs/), a Motif front end.

Scarab

Scarab (http://scarab.tigris.org) is a project to implement a bug-tracking system from the ground up. Currently, the project is pre-alpha: The database schema is being defined, and a GUI mockup has been created. Scarab is to be implemented as Java servlets.

Teacup

Teacup (www.altara.org/teacup.html) is a Web-based trouble-ticketing system. It is implemented in Perl, with a PostgresSQL back end. Teacup includes basic support for work estimation, time-tracking, and billing of work to an account.

Wrek

Wrek (www.math.duke.edu/~yu/wreq) is Web based and written in Perl 5 using gdbm as the database back end. It has a cookie-based authentication system, but htaccess and Unix passwd authentication options are also supported.

Wrek features Web and email interfaces and is designed to be distributed using a hierarchy of master and departmental servers. It is useful not only for load balancing, but, probably more importantly, to let different political/administrative groups control their own servers. It not only tracks work requests, but provides facilities for publishing FAQs and HOWTOs across the server hierarchy.

XPTS and Web/PTS

The X Problem Tracking System (www.halcyon.com/dean/pts/pts.html) is oriented toward system administration, though it is no longer under active development. It consists primarily of an X application. There is a simple text-mode and command-line interface for reporting problems.

Summary

To manage an open source project you need four kinds of software tools: an Internet clearinghouse for open source projects, a groupware system for managing the project, a version handling system to coordinate individual changes, and a problem management tool for building the software.

There are many software tools available on the Internet for managing an open source programming project. Many systems are freeware or shareware, but some also leave a few things to be desired, especially support and documentation.

CVS is by far the most popular system to help multiple users make simultaneous changes to a collection of documents and files. On the problem reporting side there is no clear winner, but Bugzilla, JitterBug, and GNU GNATS are probably the most popular.

Open Source Tool Tips

Read and you remember for a minute. Experience and you learn for life.

OLD CHINESE PROVERB

There are a lot of useful open source software and other sources around. This chapter presents a collection of some of the more useful products. The compilation is not complete by any means; it is a collection of those tools and resources we have found useful or simply interesting in working with open source projects.

Software

A good way to learn about open source is to study what others have done, and learn from their experience. In theory it should be possible to use open source as a development method for any kind of software, but in practice the majority developed is system software and programming tools. There are some interesting attempts in developing other kinds of software, but the results so far are marginal.

Open source software is not the same thing as *freeware* or *shareware*. Open source software is delivered with source code and can be modified by the user. It is also considered polite to make a contribution to the code, offer advice or possible solutions to problems found, and the like.

Amanda

The Advanced Maryland Automatic Network Disk Archiver (AMANDA) (www.amanda.org) is a backup system that allows the administrator of a LAN to set up a single master backup server to back up multiple hosts to a single large capacity tape drive.

Apache

Apache (www.apache.org) is an award-winning open source Web server.

The Apache Project

The Apache Project is a collaborative software development effort aimed at creating a robust, commercial-grade, freely available source code implementation of an HTTP (Web) server with many features. The project is jointly managed by a group of volunteers located around the world, using the Internet and the Web to communicate, plan, and develop the server and its related documentation. These volunteers are known as the Apache Group. In addition, hundreds of users have contributed ideas, code, and documentation to the project.

The Apache Group

The Apache Group is the group of individuals that was initially formed in 1995 to develop the Apache HTTP Server. The Apache Software Foundation (ASF) is a membership-based, not-for-profit corporation. Individuals who have demonstrated a commitment to collaborative open-source software development, through sustained participation and contributions within the Foundation's projects, are eligible for membership in the ASF.

The Apache Development Process

There is a core group of contributors informally called the *core*, which was formed from the project founders and is augmented from time to time when core members nominate outstanding contributors and the rest of the core members agree. The core group focus is more on business issues and limited-circulation things like security problems than on mainstream code development. The term *The Apache Group* technically refers to this core of project contributors.

The Apache Group is a meritocracy—the more work you have done, the more you are allowed to do. The group founders set the original rules, but they can be changed by vote of the active members. There is a group of people who have logins on the development server and access to the CVS repository. Everyone has access to the CVS snapshots. Changes to the code are proposed on the mailing list and usually voted on by active members. Three yes votes or no votes, or vetoes, are needed to commit a code change during a release cycle. Docs are usually committed first and then changed as needed, with conflicts resolved by majority vote. Anyone on the mailing list can vote on a particular issue, but we only count those made by active members or people who are known to be experts on that part of the server. Vetoes must be accompanied by a convincing explanation.

The primary method of communication is through the Apache mailing list. Approximately 40 messages a day flow over the list, and are typically very conversational in tone. The discussion is about new features to add, bug fixes, user problems, developments in the Web server community, release dates, and so forth.

The actual code development takes place on the developers' local machines, with proposed changes communicated using a patch (output of a unified *diff -u oldfile newfile* command), and committed to the source repository by one of the core developers using remote CVS.

New members of the Apache Group are added when one member nominates a frequent contributor, and he or she is unanimously approved by the voting members. In most cases, this new member has been actively contributing to the group's work for over six months.

Apache exists to provide a robust and commercial-grade reference implementation of the HTTP protocol. It must remain a platform upon which individuals and institutions can build reliable systems, both for experimental purposes and for mission-critical purposes.

The Apache team believes the tools of online publishing should be in the hands of everyone, and software companies should make their money providing value-added services such as specialized modules and support, among other things. They realize that it is often seen as an economic advantage for one company to "own" a market—in the software industry that means to control tightly a particular conduit such that all others must pay. Owning the protocols through which companies conduct business at the expense of all those other companies typically does this. To the extent that the protocols of the World Wide Web remain unbound by a single company, the Web will remain a level playing field for companies large and small. Thus, "ownership" of the protocol must be prevented, and the existence of a robust reference implementation of the protocol, available absolutely for free to all companies, is a tremendously good thing.

Furthermore, Apache is an organic entity; those who benefit from it by using it often contribute back to it by providing feature enhancements, bug fixes, and support for others in public newsgroups. The amount of effort expended by any particular individual is usually fairly light, but the resulting product is made very strong. This kind of community can only happen with free-ware—when someone pays for software, they usually aren't willing to fix its bugs. One can argue, then, that Apache's strength comes from the fact that it's free, and if it were not free it would suffer tremendously, even if that money were spent on a real development team.

The mission is to see Apache used very widely—by large companies, small companies, research institutions, schools, individuals, in the intranet environment, everywhere—even though this may mean that companies who could afford commercial software, and would pay for it without blinking, might get a free ride by using Apache.

Boa

Boa (www.boa.org) is a single-tasking HTTP server. That means that unlike traditional Web servers, it does not fork for each incoming connection, nor does it fork many copies of itself to handle multiple connections.

Cvsweb

Cvsweb (http://stud.fh-heilbronn.de/~zeller/cgi/cvsweb.cgi) is a script that allows easy viewing of live CVS repositories.

Grap

Grap (www.leonine.com/~ltemplin) is a wrapper designed to verify commands before executing them.

IPVS

Virtual server is a scalable and highly available server built on a cluster of real servers (www.linuxvitualserver.org). The architecture of the cluster is transparent to end users, and the users see only a single virtual server.

GNU Mailman

Mailman (www.list.org) is software to help manage email discussion lists, much like Majordomo and Smartmail. Unlike most similar products, Mailman gives each mailing list a Web page, and allows users to subscribe, unsubscribe, and so on over the Web.

mod_ssl

The mod_ssl project (www.modssl.org) provides strong cryptography for the Apache 1.3 Web server via the Secure Sockets Layer (SSL v2/v3) and Transport Layer Security (TLS v1) protocols with the help of the Open Source SSL/TLS toolkit OpenSSL, which is based on SSLeay from Eric A. Young and Tim J. Hudson.

MySQL

MySQL (www.mysql.com) is a true multi-user, multithreaded SQL database server. Structured Query Language (SQL) is the most popular and standardized database language in the world. MySQL is a client/server implementation that consists of a server daemon mysqld and many different client programs and libraries.

PHP

PHP (www.php.net) is a server-side, cross-platform, HTML-embedded scripting language.

Python

Python (www.python.org) is an interpreted, interactive, object-oriented programming language. It incorporates modules, exceptions, dynamic typing, very high level dynamic data types, and classes. Python combines remarkable power with very clear syntax. It has interfaces to many system calls and libraries, as well as to various window systems, and is extensible in C or C++. It is also usable as an extension language for applications that need a programmable interface. Finally, Python is portable: It runs on many brands of Unix, on the Mac, and on PCs under MS-DOS, Windows, Windows NT, and OS/2.

Red Hat Linux

Red Hat Linux (www.redhat.com) is a powerful, extremely stable, next-generation computer operating system that provides a high-performance computing environment for both server and desktop PCs.

SSH

Secure Shell (SSH) (www.ssh.fi) is a program that allows you to open an encrypted connection to another computer. It allows remote execution of command and copying of files from one machine to another.

Zope

Zope (www.zope.org) is a generic discussion and application server written in Python, with both search and database functions built in including an SQL back end.

Knowledge Base Systems

Knowledge base systems can be, at a minimum, glorified, automated FAQs. Fancier versions include an integrated search index that lists the FAQ contents first and mailing list archive hits and/or bug database contents last.

The basic idea behind a knowledge base is to automate customer support by organizing product support information into an easy-to-find, easy-to-access format. The knowledge base can be used by customer support personnel to find answers to common customer complaints, or can be put out on the Web, allowing the customer to do their own searching. Alternately these systems can be used to organize product info for salespeople, allowing faster or easier access to a wide range of product data for pre-sales support. At a bare minimum, a knowledge base might be an indexed set of FAQs and mailing list archives indexed with a good search engine. At the high end, the system would have ways of removing obsolete information, and be integrated with call-tracking or bug-tracking systems.

KnowledgeKit

KnowledgeKit (www.zope.org/Members/Bill/Products/KnowledgeKit) is a Zope extension that includes support for FAQ moderation and support data (for example, embedded images). Note that Zope sites tend to be visually elegant; I assume this property carries over to KnowledgeKit as well.

Faq-O-Matic

Faq-O-Matic (www.dartmouth.edu/~john/ff-serve/cache/1.html) is a Web-based system for maintaining a FAQ that includes a permission system to control that is allowed to submit updates. It is implemented as a set of Perl CGI-bin scripts.

TWiki

TWiki (http://twicki.sourceforge.net) is a Web-based collaborative discussion and document creation manager. Users can freely edit or create new Web pages using a simple markup language. Linking and embedding is automated, thus simplifying the editing. The system includes search facilities. A checkbox/radio button/pull-down menu interface can be created using the "categories" concept. The history of changes/updates to a page can be easily browsed. TWiki lacks any security or moderation facilities, so you must trust your users. It is implemented as a set of perl cgi-bins with a flat-file backend.

Enterprise Resource Planning

Enterprise Resource Planning (ERP) systems have a way of promising "all of the above." This is the market for the big software dinosaurs like SAP and Computer Associates. Usually ERP systems are a collection of tools and libraries that in principle can be configured and modified to create any of the preceding systems. They often include a financial subsystem. This allows, for example, a customer's bug report or phone call to be turned into an invoice or purchase order, which is then routed (using workflow) to the loading dock, and so on.

ERP systems are meant to be highly configurable so that they can be modified to fit any customer's business practices, but they tend to be big and difficult to configure and modify, and usually require high-priced consultants and months, if not years, of effort to deploy.

It is often the case that ERP systems don't do as good a job, or are as easy to use, as single-use tools such as the ones just listed. On the other hand, ERP systems offer a uniform, integrated meld of all of the preceding systems, which normally can't be made to play nice together.

GNU Enterprise

GnuE (www.gnue.org) is a young project hoping to create an open source ERP package. It has a variety of active developers and several projects underway, but is still in early stages. Current work focuses on a forms designer and an object/application server. The form designer allows user interfaces to be quickly defined and created for Windows, Macintosh, Motif, gtk, java/swing and ncurses. The object server defines a data abstraction layer, allowing data that come from a variety of sources such as SQL databases like Oracle, mySQL, Informix, and similar. Modules include GnueF, the forms designer, which uses wxwindows, an open source library to provide motif, gtk, win32, and mac GUIs, and has its own Java and ncurses interface builders. libgda is a transaction manager/data access library. It provides a data abstraction interface to SQL databases. GEAS is the GnuE object server.

Open Source ERP

Open Source ERP (www.opensourceerp.org) can be interesting, but currently it is only vaporware. There is no code available yet, but the specifications look quite interesting. If the product shows up and the developers keep their promise, it could be a very interesting piece of software.

Panther/POSSL

POSSL (www.possl.org) is an open source version of an established commercial ERP package. The license, Jyacc Public License, appears to be BSD-like in nature. Although a large chunk of Panther has been opened, it's not clear which parts. Panther seems to consist of a transaction manager that provides access to various databases, a screen definition system that will create user interfaces for windows, Java, and HTTP. The system includes a GUI designer and an object repository.

Other Resources

We might all be more successful if we followed the advice we give to others. There is a lot of free advice on open source on the Internet, like discussion groups, communities, and Web magazines.

The FreeBSD Project

FreeBSD's home page can be found at www.freebsd.org.

FreeBSD 'Zine

The FreeBSD 'Zine site (www.reebsdzine.org) contains information about the open source in general, and freeBSD in particular.

Freshmeat

Freshmeat (http://freshmeat.net) maintains the largest index of Linux software on the Web. The first stop for Linux users hunting for the software they need for work or play, Freshmeat is continuously updated with the latest news from the "release early, release often" community. In addition to providing news on new releases, Freshmeat offers a variety of original content on technical, political, and social aspects of software and programming written by both Freshmeat readers and Free Software luminaries. The comment board attached to each article serves as a home for spirited discussion, bug reports, and technical support.

First Monday

First Monday (www.firstmonday.dk) is one of the first peer-reviewed magazines.

Linux.com

Linux.com's mission is to enrich the Linux community by providing a centralized place for individuals of all experience levels to learn and teach the power and virtues of the Linux Operating System.

Linux.com is an international effort by a dedicated group of coders, layout and graphics artists, writers, and network and system administrators who like Linux. The site aims to provide the Linux community with the central gathering place it has lacked for so long and to promote the use of Linux far and wide. To that end, Linux.com contains a wealth of articles, support information, columns, links, a Lug database, and more.

Linux.com employs seven full-time and two part-time staff members, most of whom serve in management positions. The volunteer staff generates the bulk of the site's content.

Linux.org

Linux.org is a Linux information site, similar to linux.com (but East Coast U.S., rather than West Coast U.S.).

Open Content

Open Content (www.opencontent.org) is an advocacy and licensing site for open documentation.

Open Source

The Open Source Initiative's Web site can be found at www.opensource.org.

154 **CHAPTER 9**

Summary

A good way to learn about open source is to study what others have done. There is a lot to learn from other open source projects and Internet resources. The list of resources is constantly changing, but you can get technical advice on how to build the software from Linux communities and Web magazines.

The next chapter will deal with issues of how to set up an open source project.

CHAPTER 10

Setting Up an Open Source Project

In the beginning there was sex. Then there was violence. Then there was apocalypse. And finally there was shopping. Such has been the narrative— part Old Testament, part old Judith Krantz—of the Internet thus far. But in truth we ain't seen nothin' yet, and much of our national conversation to date about the Internet, especially that to be found in the mainstream media-political culture, is not keeping up with the pace of change.

FRANK RICH, "THE FUTURE WILL RESUME IN 15 DAYS," *NEW YORK TIMES*, DECEMBER 18, 1999

Open source software does not work because "the whole Internet has become your research and development and quality assurance department" (or for other reasons you may have read in the news). The amount of talented programmers available for any set of tasks is limited. All open source projects compete for limited resources (the interest of the available programmers).

Motivations for Open Source

In addition to the political and ideological issues behind open source, the business issue is speed, or faster time-to-market. For example, the company VA Linux Systems thrives upon the success of open source software in general. They sell Linux systems, installed with myriad open source tools and applications, to clients that require enterprise-ready components and software. They also sell support for these systems. If the selection and quality of open source software improves, VA Linux Systems can offer its customers more competitive solutions.

Open source is not charity. Charity is designed to offer a resource to a defined group of people who are perceived as "in need." Open projects provide their offerings to anyone who wants them, and project participants usually come from the community being served. Open projects' participants can be motivated by charity, but the scope of the projects is wider than that of most charities.

Some people participate in open source projects because they believe it's their civic duty. Some are motivated charitably. Some do so as a hobby. Others do so to enhance their reputations in the community. Many people who participate in open projects use their offerings on a daily basis and want the advantages of community-wide feedback on their quality and usability. This is a very common motivation for people who participate in open projects involving computer software.

There are as many reasons to participate in open projects, as there are people. Many of the motivations involve personal gain. There is no general political viewpoint associated with open source. Because many people participate in these projects for personal gain, or as a hobby, participants come from a broad spectrum of political viewpoints. But some people are led to participate by their political philosophies. A socialist might see open projects as a desirable allocation of public resources. A libertarian might see open project activity as a new sort of "transfinite" free market. There's quite a bit of diversity in the community.

The mechanism for business success is choice and efficiency. In the open source network economy, value is no longer created in a sequence, but also in parallel. In open source projects, people work and collaborate synchronously, asynchronously, and semisynchronously. We are shifting from a linear economy to a network economy.

An open source company does not need much start-up capital either to become established or to expand. It simply establishes a virtual link over the Internet to the competence it requires. This is usually done in a clearinghouse for open source projects, like SourceForge, Open Projects Net, or Slashdot. These are key online social centers for the open source community, as they provide a centralized place for open source developers to control and manage open source software development. They post several articles each day on topics of interest to the community.

There is no need to own all the resources when you can simply collaborate with others online. The virtual enterprise can expand with few employees and with limited investments. Instead, the risks are spread among the members of the established virtual network. While the legal units may be small, the network as a whole may be huge.

Open Source Methodology

There is no single open source methodology; many forms of development are used. Many open source projects have a single project leader who coordinates development. But some, like Apache, use a team approach to management with no single leader. Many open source projects will post new code regularly to the source tree. Others only post changed sources every few days or weeks.

Nonetheless, the last decade has seen an obvious trend toward outsourcing and networks as a new model for conducting business on any scale. *Virtual companies*, *supply chains*, and *value networks* have become essential terms of the Internet economy. As Christopher Meyer, Director of the Ernst & Young Center for Business Innovation wrote in his 1997 report, "The Connected Economy: Beyond the Information Age":

> As the connected economy emerges, enterprises are recognizing that the interactions among economic actors have become at least as important as the efficient functioning of each agent... The actions of one agent affect the choices of another, so they are connected. Simulations with large numbers of interacting agents show that they behave in ways that are often unpredictable; the properties of such systems are said to 'emerge' from the behavior of the connected individuals.

It is impossible to predict, of course, the precise business model that will predominate. There is no doubt, however, that the traditional model of the company is already well along the way toward evolving into the connected enterprise.

Closed source business (as opposed to open source) builds their business model on owning the technology. They own the right to the Application Programming Interfaces (APIs, a collection of software routines and interfaces) and the standards. The best example is Microsoft, which owns their programming interface Win32. Anyone who intends to write a program for Microsoft Windows must use this API.

This business model called *lock-in* is used to compete with other companies. It works deliberately against every other company who owns similar but competing APIs. Competitors might have better technology, better services or lower costs, but are unable to use these benefits, as they don't have access to the platform. Customers become reliant on the platform and must pay a large cost for switching to a different platform.

IT users are notoriously subject to switching costs and lock-in. Once you have chosen a technology, or a format for keeping information, switching can be very expensive. Most of us have experienced the costs of switching from one brand of software to another: data files are unlikely to transfer perfectly, incompatibilities with other tools often arise, and, most important, retraining is required.

Having a choice does not just mean having the freedom to choose, but the freedom to choose from various affordable solutions. Switching costs are significant, and CIOs think long and hard about changing systems. Lock-in to historical, legacy systems is commonplace in the network economy. Such lock-in is not absolute—new technologies do displace old ones—but switching costs can dramatically alter companies' strategies and options. In fact, the magnitude of switching costs is itself a strategic choice made by the producer of the system.

Lock-in arises whenever users invest in multiple complementary and durable assets specific to a particular IT system. You purchased a bunch of Apple Macintosh computers as well as software. So long as these assets were valuable—the computers still worked and the software did its job—you had less reason to buy new PCs and start buying expensive LANs and Windows programs.

More generally, in replacing an old system with a new, incompatible one, you may find it necessary to swap out or duplicate all the components of your system. These components typically include a range of assets like data files, various pieces of durable hardware, and training or human capital. Switching from Apple to Intel equipment involves not only new hardware, but also new software. Also, the knowledge that you and your employees have built up that enables you to use your hardware and software must be updated. The switching costs for changing computer systems can be astronomical. Today's state-of-the-art choice is tomorrow's legacy system.

Switching costs can be minimized if switching software does not necessitate switching platforms. Thus it is always in a customer's interest to demand that the software they deploy be based on open systems platforms.

This type of situation is the norm in the information economy. A company that has selected a special technology and architecture for its networking needs will find it very costly to change to an incompatible network technology. Whether the enterprise is locked into proprietary "closed source" products or to an "open" standard with multiple suppliers can make a big difference.

Reference bodies of open source software that implement a communications protocol or API are more important to the long-term life of that platform then several independent *closed source* implementations. Commercial software can always be bought by a competitor, which can discontinue the product. Consequently closed source products can never be independent.

Lock-in can occur on an individual level, a company level, or even a national level. Many consumers were locked into LP libraries, at least in the sense that they were less inclined to purchase CD players because they could not play LPs. Many companies were locked into Lotus 1-2-3 spreadsheets because their employees were highly trained in using the Lotus command structure. Lotus even sued Borland for copying the 1-2-3 command structure in its spreadsheet Quattro Pro, a dispute that went all the way to the Supreme Court. Today, at a national level, most of us are locked into Microsoft's Windows desktop operating environment.

In competing to become the standard, or at least to achieve critical mass, consumer expectations are critical. In a very real sense, the product that is expected to become the standard will become the standard. Self-fulfilling expectations are one manifestation of positive-feedback economics and bandwagon effects. As a result, companies participating in markets with strong network effects seek to convince customers that their products will ultimately become the standard, while rival, incompatible products will soon be orphaned.

Very often, support for a new technology can be assembled in the context of a formal standard-setting effort. If you own valuable intellectual property but need to gain critical mass, you must decide whether to promote your technology unilaterally, in the hope that it will become a de facto standard that you can tightly control, or to make various openness commitments to help achieve a critical mass. Adobe followed an openness strategy with its page description language, PostScript, explicitly allowing other software houses to implement PostScript interpreters, because they realized that such widespread use helped establish a standard.

Some open source projects place restrictions on who can use their offerings. Such restrictions make a project less open. Other projects restrict how their offerings may be used, which also makes their projects less open. Openness is a matter of degree.

It may be tempting to save a failed project by giving away the source code. Netscape, the one-time darling of the stock market, offers a good example of how economic principles can serve as an early warning system. The code must be runnable. The source code to their Netscape Navigator was released at Mozilla.org in March 1998, but the initial release was not running code, and interest from users faded away. So far Mozilla has not created any new Web browser at all. Three important questions to ask are:

> To what degree does the product implement a new platform?

> What are the business interests in maintaining ownership of that platform?

> How much of the revenue comes from the platform and how much comes from products and services?

The company that best understands information systems and complementary products will be best positioned to move rapidly and aggressively. Netscape grabbed the Web browser market early on by giving away its product. It lost money on every sale but made up for it in volume. Netscape was able to give away its browser and sell it, too, by bundling such critical components as customer support with the retail version and by selling complementary goods such as server software for hefty prices. But Netscape failed. Netscape was fundamentally vulnerable because its chief competitor, Microsoft, controls the operating environment of which a Web browser is but one component.

Netscape faced a classic problem of interconnection: Its browser needed to work in conjunction with Microsoft's operating system. Local telephone companies battling the Bell System around 1900 faced a similar dependency upon their chief rival when they tried to interconnect with Bell to offer long-distance service. Many did not survive. Interconnection battles have arisen regularly over the past century in the telephone, the railroad, the airline, and the computer industries, among others.

All software cannot be developed open source. Open source software tends to concentrate on infrastructural and back-end software. Open source benefits from incremental design, which means back-end systems. End-user applications are hard to write. These applications deal with graphical user interfaces, which are very complex to write, almost always customized, and comprise other skills like graphical interface design.

Culturally, open source software has been done in networking code and operating systems for a long time. Much open source software was written by engineers to solve a technical problem while developing commercial software. The primary audience is other engineers.

This is why open source software consists of mainly operating systems and development tools and not desktop programs, with some notable exceptions like the Adobe Photoshop-like Gimp or GNU Image Manipulation Program. (Gimp is also a platform since it has a plug-in architecture.)

Open source companies can thus expect to evolve further into something else, based upon the results of their network connections. In fact, communication is the primary value of open source.

Satisfying developers is probably the most challenging issue in open source development. Developers must feel that they are giving good contributions to the project and getting a reward or a very good explanation as to why the effort was not integrated into the distribution. Their concerns must be addressed, and their comments to the architecture and design must be acknowledged and respected.

Build a Team

Millions have flocked to the Net in an incredibly short time, not because it was user-friendly—it wasn't—but because it seemed to offer some intangible quality long missing in action from modern life. The Internet connected people to each other and provided a space in which the human voice would be rapidly rediscovered.

R. Levine, C. Locke, D. Searls, and D. Weinberger,
The Cluetrain Manifesto, **Perseus Books, 2000**

Teams of people conduct open source work. The days of the individual contributor working in blissful (or bored) isolation may be numbered. In the open source economy, all work is project work—and you are your projects.

In every organization, teams of employees are working together on projects of all types: ad hoc and regularly planned, crisis-driven and seasonal, customer-facing and internal in nature. The Internet has made these teams relatively easy to form across time and geography, and is increasingly relied upon to improve the performance of those teams.

Teams increasingly include outside members: specialty firms, independent contractors, temporary employees, and so forth. This has become practical in large part because these freelance team members enjoy the appropriate level of access to information and to other team members as if they were actual employees.

But these external freelancers increase the need for better communication tools. Real-time, person-to-person communication like video conferencing is essential to improve the efficiency of the team's work. As capabilities improve, they allow the virtual environment to develop. Instead of exchanging text by email or chat, we'll be working at different and more effective levels of abstraction, closer to the way we do in the physical world. In the emerging virtual environments, we will interact more effectively with open source.

Relationships will naturally continue to rely on face-to-face and physical contact, on shared experience and values, on acts of generosity and thoughtfulness, and on trust, understanding, and empathy. Nevertheless, open source has the potential to have significant, fundamental impact on the types of relationships we maintain and on how we conceive of time. Thomas W. Malone and Robert J. Laubacher wrote in "The Dawn of the E-Lance Economy" (Harvard Business Review, September 1998):

> As communications technologies advance and networks become more efficient, the shift to e-lancers promises to accelerate. Should that indeed take place, the dominant business organization of the future may not be a stable, permanent corporation but rather an elastic network that may sometimes exist for no more than a day or two. When a project needs to be undertaken, requests for proposals will be transmitted or electronic want ads posted, individuals or small teams will respond, a network will be formed, and new workers will be brought on as their particular skills are needed. Once the project is done, the network will disband.

We see these ways of working—synchronously, asynchronously, or parallel/linear—which had been offered as separate tools, starting to merge and blur. Because of client pressures to do so, Web-based collaboration, team, or office suites now offer both synchronous-like chat and asynchronous-like email, document storage and scheduling functions in the same tool.

Unfortunately, the features and functionality that make software flexible are often the same factors that reduce its performance and reliability and increase its cost. A deluxe Swiss army knife that includes every possible function and feature is more likely to be unwieldy to carry, have more pieces that break, and to be more than is needed in many situations. However, a single blade may not be enough. Increasing features and functionality in the Swiss army knife mean adding more metal. In a software product, increased features mean an increased number of functional specifications, which require an increased number of programming engineers to develop them, and an increased number of potential points of failure, that is, blades that may break.

More and more of these functions are also bundled as suites, for example, Internet Office (www.integratedapps.com), ThoughtStar with QuickTeam (www.quickteam.com), Lotus Notes (www.lotus.com), Centrinity First Class (www.centriniy.com), and Groove by Groove Networks (www.groove.com).

The days of large Notes installations with dedicated personnel, servers, and complex, difficult-to-master applications are going away. Today, the trend is toward a browser-based client, ease-of-use, and little or no training required. Furthermore, many of the new offerings are on an Application Service Provider (ASP). This takes many of the in-house costs and outsources them, allowing users to get started faster and with less cost and risk. Because cost and learning curve have been two of the biggest barriers to electronic collaboration (education being the third), this new ASP model is changing the land-scape and acceptance level of electronic collaboration quite radically.

Technology is not enough. Although the technology is getting better, and the distribution channels more efficient, a real problem with electronic collaboration is still not being well addressed. That problem does not always have a technical solution because the obstacle is how people interact with each other through the software. It is a sociotechnical as well as a technical issue. Very few organizations think of collaboration as strategic. More enlightened organizations see collaboration as a competitive advantage and a way to overcome time and distance for a global presence. These organizations are demanding software that deals with both people and technology. People want to collaborate anytime and anywhere. With the emergence of standards such as Wireless Access Protocol (WAP), for mobile Internet applications, we expect to see mobile collaborative applications emerging.

Successful projects provide opportunities for personal and career growth, pay close attention to motivation and incentive factors, and have the appropriate levels of organizational support and visibility. The primary success factor is the project team and its ability to successfully communicate, cooperate, and collaborate with the project stakeholders. In a distributed team environment, the key success factor is the quality of the virtual team.

Using groupware, videoconferencing, and other collaborative technologies, virtual teams are bridging time, space, and organizational barriers. The conventional way in which people work is coming unglued.

As important as positive relationships and high trust are in all teams, they are even more important in virtual ones. The lack of daily face-to-face time, offering opportunities to quickly clear things up, can heighten misunderstandings. For many distributed teams, trust has to substitute for hierarchical and bureaucratic controls. Virtual teams with high trust offer this valuable social asset back to their sponsoring organizations for use in future cooperative opportunities.

Managing distributed projects requires more advanced skills and leadership competencies. In traditional teams we can rely on the team in a shared physical space to be supportive. In a virtual team, each team member is required to apply higher levels of self-discipline and professionalism.

Virtual teams have a harder time getting started and holding together than colocated teams. Thus, they need to be much more intentional about creating face-to-face meetings that nourish the natural rhythms of team life.

Managing distributed projects requires an incredible focus on people, communication, and project leadership, and perhaps even social leadership. The project manager and team members of today and the future must learn to be "great communicators" in order to be successful.

Groupware is technology designed to facilitate the work of groups or teams, as discussed in Chapter 7, "Managing Distributed Open Source Projects." This technology may be used to communicate, cooperate, coordinate, solve problems, compete, or negotiate. While traditional technologies like the telephone qualify as groupware, the term is ordinarily used to refer to a specific class of technologies that rely on modern computer networks, such as email, newsgroups, videophones, or chat.

Clearinghouses

Clearinghouses are places where software developers call for help from other developers looking for interesting projects. The clearinghouses are only for software development, but the idea is general. For example, Openlaw (www.openlaw.org) mentioned in Chapter 3, "The Open Source Philosophy," is an experiment in creating legal argument in an open forum. With public assistance, arguments, draft pleadings, and edit briefs are crafted in public, online. Anyone can join by adding thoughts and comments on drafts in progress, and suggesting reference sources.

SourceForge

SourceForge (http://sourceforge.net) is a free hosting service for open source developers that offers, among other things, a CVS repository, mailing lists, bug tracking, message forums, task management software, Web site hosting, permanent file archival, full backups, and total Web-based administration.

SourceForge's mission is to enrich the open source community by providing a centralized place for open source developers to control and manage open source software development.

As SourceForge grows, it provides traffic to the projects hosted. There is great benefit to giving end users a window into a development environment. There will be more peer review of the source, and potential developers will be wandering by.

The individual authors hold the copyright on their own software. Because of the nature of Open Source licenses, we are allowed to give people access to that software; however, all licenses disputes and issues are the responsibilities of the individual authors. There is often a misconception that open source software does not actually have a license holder, because of its free nature. This is not the case, however, and software hosted on SourceForge is responsible for its own licensing.

No system is uncrackable, but SourceForge continuously monitors the software used for bugs and security holes, and audits the software regularly. Encryption is available and enforced on all parts of the SourceForge site except mailing lists.

Other Sites Using SourceForge

Bioinformatics.org (http://bioinformatics.org/)	Open Source software for bioinformatics
Handhelds.org (http://handhelds.org/SourceForge/)	Development clearing house and resource for handheld development
Linuxalpha (www.linuxalpha.compaq.com/sourceforge/)	Development site for Linux on Compaq Alpha microprocessor-based machines
Motifzone.org (www.motifzone.org/)	Development site of the Unix graphical user interface Motif
Open Source Directory (www.opensourcedirectory.org/)	Directory of stable Open Source software
Pennsylvania Report (www.pa-report.com/)	Home page of Political news reports
University of South Carolina (http://source.cse.sc.edu)	Home page of educational institution

Open Projects Net

Open Projects Net (http://openprojects.nu) is a work in progress, created in 1998 to promote projects and activities that involve open access to technology or information. OPN's founder Robert Levin has been head of operations for the Linux Internet Support Cooperative since 1994. Having experienced first hand the benefits of free software, Robert set out to apply those benefits to a wider world.

Open Projects Net's focus includes open source and free software applications and operating systems, open hardware, open standards, free technology, technological education, public domain advocacy, literacy, open access for the disabled, and public access to art. Its slogan sums up the focus: open source, open technology, and open information.

Slashdot

Slashdot (http://slashdot.org) publishes stories about open source projects. It is also a community for discussions about the articles with links to other sites.

When Slashdot links a site, often a lot of readers will hit the link to read the story. This is called the "Slashdot Effect" and can easily throw thousands of hits at the site in minutes. Most of the time, large professional Web sites have no problem with this, but often a site we link will be a smaller site, used to getting only a few thousand hits a day. When all those Slashdot readers start crashing the party, it can saturate the site completely, causing the site to buckle under the strain. When this happens, the site is said to be "Slashdot-ted." Recently, the terms *Slashdot Effect* and *Slashdotted* have been used more generally to refer to any short-term traffic jam at a Web site.

Summary

In order to set up an open source project you need a project that attracts motivated programmers (or others). There are as many reasons to participate in open projects as there are people. Many of these motivations involve personal gain. Developers must feel that they are giving good contributions to the project and getting a reward or a very good explanation as to why the effort was not integrated into the distribution.

There is no single open source methodology. Many open source projects have a single project leader who coordinates development. But some, like Apache, use a team approach to management with no single leader. Many open source projects will post new code regularly; others only occasionally.

Don't put any restrictions on the use of the code. It makes a project less open. Also, it may be tempting to save a failed project by giving away the source code. But the code must be runnable. Otherwise the interest from users will fade away.

CHAPTER 11

Open Source Management Anecdotes

Pablo Picasso once said that good art is created, but great art is stolen. On the Internet, the same holds true. Good code is created, but great code is copied over and over.

CARL MALAMUD, MEDIA.ORG, HTTP://PUBLIC.RESOURCE.ORG/

Most open source packages have their roots as a hobby project. People pick it up and extend or modify the code. This kind of voluntary and *organic* development has a lot of strengths, but it is also volatile. For example, a well-documented design is not an open source strength. As a result, programmers have to rely on guesswork, folklore, and reverse engineering if they want to understand how many of these projects work.

Open source is also a mixture of political ideas and business opportunities never seen before in modern business. Therefore, it is important to understand the underlying forces behind open source. This chapter contains a collection of anecdotes to illustrate these forces. I hope it will serve both to inform and guide further development of open source projects, and to show novices what to think about before, during, and after they start an open source project.

Open Aid to Developing Countries

Open source software directly influences the global economy by making third world countries more competitive, for example, the Indian and Mexican software industry. Open source software doesn't cost more than a few dollars for a CD, or via the Internet, can be freely distributed.

I was the moderator of the conference "Component Computing" in Sweden in 1999. During a session break I had a discussion concerning Linux, and heard the following story (unfortunately I cannot remember the name of the source):

> I met this guy, a minister at the Mexican government. He had received a truckload of money from the UN and Unesco. He was responsible for a project to provide 140,000 schools with computer networks. First he called Microsoft and got an offer on Windows NT worth 150 M USD. But then he had a second thought: "Hmm... I'd better check the Internet." He found a distributor of Linux and bought a CD for fifty bucks on his personal credit card. Then he said to me: "150 million dollars or 50 bucks? It's a no-brainer!"

In some European countries, like France, the Ministries of Education have taken steps in supporting Linux, but nowhere is the education revolution stronger than in Mexico. They are with their Scholar Net program installing a nation-wide network of computer laboratories using open software like Linux and Gnome. Over the next few years, they will be installing 140,000 laboratories at a rate of 20,000 to 35,000 per year. Each lab will train a number of students in Linux and open source, at least indirectly. Suddenly, a low-salary country like Mexico can offer a million highly educated Linux programmers and skilled Linux users. Without any judgments, this is a true revolution in the IT industry that will have a great impact on the market.

Let's give this a second thought. Actually, this situation is not unique. Most of the technologies that make the Web possible are open source. Bind, the program that runs the DNS, is the single most mission critical Internet application. According to the market survey company Netcraft (www.netcraft.co.uk), more that 50 percent of all Web sites run open source Apache Web server. Open source tools like Perl and Python generate the majority of the Web sites. Virtually every vendor's TCP/IP stack (including Microsoft's) is based on one originally developed as part of the open source Berkeley Unix networking package. Most of the commercial XML packages build on the open source XML parser written by James Clark, an independent programmer living in Thailand who also wrote many of the GNU text-processing tools.

Even the Largest Sites Use Open Source

In the early days of Unix and the Internet, programmers routinely shared their source code. AT&T was prohibited from competing in the computer industry, so Ken Thompson and Dennis Ritchie sent out Unix source tapes from Bell Labs for a nominal copying fee. Hundreds, then thousands of programmers built on their work, contributing individual utilities, porting the software to additional platforms, and in general doing whatever it took to make the software meet their own unique needs. The result was mission-critical quality software used by even the largest companies.

David Filo, cofounder of Yahoo!, told the story of Yahoo! in FreeBSD News, Issue 1. The search engine began its life at Stanford University on a commercial Unix system. But he found that the system was not designed to be a scalable HTTP server. He tried a number of commercial systems, but none was suitable in terms of performance and stability. By chance he tried the Unix-like open source operating system FreeBSD. A couple of days later he added a FreeBSD box to the Yahoo! cluster of Web servers. Not only did it outperform the rest of the machines, but it was more stable. Although the price was certainly attractive, it was the stability, performance, and access to the source code that that settled the matter. Ever since then Yahoo! used FreeBSD almost exclusively for production as well as the development environment.

The Internet itself with key technologies like TCP/IP and DNS were and are still developed through the open source process. The Internet Engineering Task Force (IETF) defines the open standards that make the Internet possible. Much of the work is done via mailing lists, with face-to-face working group meetings held three times a year. Anyone on the Internet can join the mailing lists or come to the meetings, as the IETF is a bottom-up standards body. Sometimes an Area Director identifies problems and asks people to volunteer solutions. More often, Working Groups are simply formed by interested people getting together and asking to be recognized. Competing solutions are evaluated on their technical merits with a focus on simplicity and interoperability. As with any successful open source project, there is a fundamental vision, mostly articulated by the Internet Architecture Board, which guides the effort. But some central authority does not appoint these chairmen and architectural visionaries. They emerge and are subsequently chosen by their peers through their almost always irregular search for optimal solutions. Tim O'Reilly quoted Admiral Grace Hopper, inventor of Cobol, in Release 1.0, Edventure Holdings (November 1998) by saying:

> To me programming is more than an important practical art. It is also a gigantic undertaking in the foundations of knowledge.

But looking at just the best-known packages misses the point. When you scrape the surface, open source software is everywhere. To me it is clear: All future networked information applications will be based on open source technology. Proprietary material always costs money. If the alternative is gratis and features are free to copy, proprietary technology simply is no alternative (given that the quality of the free content is sufficient, of course). Also the specifications for creating documents and content are simple, open, and clearly documented. There are, for example, many free archives of useful Java, Perl, Tcl, Python, HTML, and XML scripts. As the number of free tools increases, the knowledge among the users increases dramatically.

Scientific results build on replication. One scientist cannot expect to account for all possible test conditions, nor necessarily have the test environment to fully test every aspect of a hypothesis. By sharing hypotheses and results with a community of peers, the scientist enables many eyes to see what one pair of eyes might miss.

Open source has the same two-part development model—free sharing of information and free sharing of results. The sharing of source code developers makes software more robust. Programs get used and tested in a wider variety of contexts than one programmer could generate, and bugs get uncovered that otherwise would not be found. Companies developing proprietary software partly use this method. It is common to publish free, but not open source, "beta releases" and get bug reports in response.

The other part, open sharing of results, also facilitates discovery. The scientific method minimizes duplication of effort because peers will know when they are working on similar projects. Progress does not stop simply because one scientist stops working on a project. If the results are worthy, other scientists will follow up. Similarly in the open source development model, sharing source code facilitates creativity. Anyone can use the results of the other or combine resources into a single project. One project may provide the inspiration for another project. And worthy projects need not be orphaned when the creator moves on. With information like a source code available, others can step in and take over.

Time Is the Critical Factor in Open Source

My dad likes the Internet. But he doesn't surf the Net, he only uses email. That's his impression of the Internet. The new "killer application" is not another Office Suite, or a competitor to Windows, or Internet, or the Web.

It is true that there is no "free lunch." Somebody must pay with something, money or time. But for the ordinary private user, time is not a cost as it is in the industry. If something is "free" and you "pay" with time, support or adaptation of software for example, open source is truly free. Open source software gives anyone the tool to use the Internet, that is, to communicate. It's sites like C I Net, Amazon.com, and Yahoo! It's also communication itself. It's the nearness to information and the opportunity to interact with others.

Email and chat enable people to communicate and to build relationships. As people are social beings we have a social need to communicate; we communicate for its own sake. Thus all inventions that simplify the means of communication—that eliminate time and distance—will by definition be a success like the telephone. Successful sites like C | Net, Amazon.com, and Yahoo! not only produce good information, but they also communicate with their customers. They do not necessarily ask the customers questions, but carefully observe the customers' needs, which is communication. The result is better service. The Internet is not about system solutions and well-designed sites. The first thing visitors see when they come to a site is how it will service them. That service is how companies build their brands and create an audience. The systems solutions and design become important only after the user accepts the marketing, ideology, branding, audience development, and communication platform that are set for the site.

What has this got to do with open source? The answer is that open source is forcing a deeper paradigm shift in the computer industry. With Internet and open source the shift in value creating in IT business is from software to content, as the desktop no longer is Windows but the Web browser. Also, as in all paradigm shifts, the entry barriers to the market are low. Thus open source won't beat Microsoft in its own field, but by changing the very nature of the game. Open source software will not replace Microsoft, but instead it will create a new market. Source code is available for independent peer review. You cannot only try a new product for free, but also build your own customized version of it. It is possible to add a feature, subtract a feature, or change a feature, and more importantly, because open source focuses on solving real problems, there is room for experimentation in an environment that is not market driven.

Unlike some open source advocates, I don't like to single out Microsoft as the great enemy. But the company's attempt to improve the Web with their proprietary ActiveX controls is a good example of the paradigm shift in the IT industry. ActiveX tools was an excellent, expensive technology aimed at professional programmers, and could not easily be copied and implemented by ordinary users. Microsoft has an enormous interest in protecting their investments and keeping the status quo. This makes it difficult for them to embrace (or maybe even to understand) anything really new, and allows new players to create new markets. Figuratively speaking, open source appears to make anyone a competitor to Microsoft.

With a little perspective this has happened earlier in history, when IBM gave away the market to Microsoft because IBM didn't see that the shift of power was not only from the mainframe to the PC, but also from proprietary to commodity, and from hardware to software. Part of leading Linux distributor

Red Hat's success is due to the lower costs in adapting software to specialized needs. Proprietary licenses create a barrier to entry because of the requirement for negotiation and agreement. In practice Linux gives developers real control over the operating system layer in the technology they are using. This is much like the control that IBM gave computer buyers when they published the specifications to the original IBM PC. Open source developers take command and get an increased choice over closed systems and limited choice. This control enables them to build more reliable, stable, and secure systems at a lower cost than the proprietary binary-only alternatives. Open source is an efficient way of getting developers to work on features that matter, tools that the builders need. Behind the scene of C | Net, Amazon.com, and Yahoo! are many developers and administrators who are continually rebuilding the product. These sites, which are the world's largest and most successful Web sites, run entirely on open source software: FreeBSD, Linux, Apache, Tcl, Python, and Perl.

Summary

It is important not to forget the underlying characteristics of open source. It is a tool, but it is also political. Because open source has only been around for a few years, it's no surprise we're still having a hard time figuring out exactly what it is, much less what its political implications are. It is not a matter of taking a political stand, but to understand the underlying causes to better make use of open source. Open source is a "peoples movement," growing from below. Is it not an invention of any big official company or organization. Individuals with different standpoints have developed open source. One can learn important lessons and get new perspectives from case studies and talking to people involved in open source, to get ready for open source. Which takes us to Chapter 12.

Are You Ready for Open Source?

Paradise can get tiresome; Inferno is where the action is!

DANTE

Open source is still a very young field. There are a wide variety of ideas and methods around, some with political overtones, others mainly marketing talk. The unsuccessful have not yet had enough time to fail convincingly.

Success means different things to different people and for different projects. A commercially failed project may accomplish an educational purpose. A failed project can serve as a stopgap measure until another more complete and stable product is developed to replace it.

Practical Advice

I, and a couple of other likeminded persons, founded the company Crealog in 1990. The intention was to create something that benefits from working with an open source strategy in a network environment. Essentially it is an experiment in how to build a company in a *business development network* for the *new* economy using open source strategies. We strongly believe that the open source concept can be used not only for software development, but also generally. It has to be somewhat modified, but from a general point of view any business can benefit from the advantages of working with an open source model. Working this way may not create cheaper solutions, but definitely creates smarter and more creative solutions.

I would like to give some practical advice and assistance on working with open source in a network organization, based on my experience so far.

It is difficult to make others understand why you should work in a network organization. It is even harder to get people to understand *how* you work in a network organization. You may understand the theories, but most people fail in practice. It is a waste of time trying to force them, if they are used to taking or giving orders. Open source projects and network organizations are completely different from the ordinary line organizations and value chain mind models.

To really understand the benefits and execute the work correctly are matters of insight and foresight. As open source and network organizations build on voluntary actions and freedom with responsibility, the only means of control are trust and respect, and consequently truth and openness are prerequisite. This also implies that full information flow between managers, employees, and members in the network is necessary.

Some companies and people just don't get it. For various reasons they cannot handle the freedom and responsibility needed. They cannot create the respect to build and operate in a network organization. One of the most persistent misperceptions is that people in leadership positions are leaders. By definition, leaders are simply people who have followers, and rank doesn't have much to do with that.

A successful network organization requires a well-functioning business foundation. It is very hard to work in an open source network without a solid business.

Today companies are knowledge-based. According to the management gurus Don Tapscott and Peter F. Drucker, a knowledge-based company has three basic assets: the *structural capital* (the management), the *human capital* (the employees or collaborators knowledge), and the *relational capital* (the customers' and the employees' loyalty). All these three concepts have, unlike the ordinary monetary asset, the interesting property, volatility. People are free to leave if they don't like the conditions. Customers simply don't buy from companies they don't like.

Success is measured by how carefully you manage the company's relations between employees, collaborators, partners, customers, and so on. A relation is built around trust and respect. You can earn respect and create confidence, mainly by communicating and speaking the truth. It is a condition in which you have full and deliberate straightforwardness in all relations. This sounds like a truism, but this actually is almost an exception that proves the rule. People are not evil or stupid, but we feel that traditional hierarchical line organizations in combination with poor managers often make people somewhat selfish and ignorant. People like to "improve the truth" to get personal benefits like advancements.

Selfishness is sometimes looked upon as a merit in business, as a CEO's first duty is to care for the shareholder. This is contradictory to how value is created in an open source network organization, where it is prerequisite to give something for free, in order to get something else for free. Open source is about solving problems, not looking for revenue. This raises four questions:

➤ What kind of leadership does the company practice?

➤ What does the company do to build teamwork into its way of doing business?

➤ Does the company embody social values that give it a powerful sense of purpose?

➤ How does the company integrate technology into the way its people operate? This is often a cultural clash in traditional companies.

Open Source Benefits

But for those who comprehend and utilize the open source and network mechanisms and are looking for solutions, the benefits are big. As with all problem solving, cooperation is simply the most winning strategy. And you easily find people on the Internet who will solve an interesting problem just for the fun of it.

But don't expect to get these assistants for free. All services have a price. Money is not the issue here, but a reward like eternal glory is, like education or access to the information. Community is also a reason. The sheer pleasure of working in partnership with a group of committed people working on an interesting project is a strong motivation in itself. Most open source software has been produced through decentralized, community-based development processes. These are usually open to anyone with the right skills. Users of open source products like software and information, can join development communities and participate in the refinement and improvement of the existing software or information.

Generally many open source development projects are almost model community development projects. They are based on open communication, inclusiveness, personal relationships, and working for the good of the community as a whole. In the article "Technology and Pleasure" published in the Web magazine *First Monday* issue 4.2, Gisle Hannemyr describes the history of the "hacker" community, placing it in the artisan tradition and in opposition to Taylorism. He describes its imperatives as:

> Reject hierarchies

> Mistrust authority

> Promote decentralization

> Share information

> Serve your community

It is not necessary for a company interested in trying open source methods to adapt these specific ideas to succeed, but as an example they give a pretty clear picture of what kinds of values are around. Other similar values could be to reduce dependencies on multinational corporations, to create alternatives to commercial products, or to encourage learning and experimentation.

The educational value of working with a group of experienced programmers, management consultants, or any other professional should also not be underestimated. These open source projects are a kind of informal, peer-to-peer university. A productive team increases the knowledge in the group. Just as the network becomes the computer, so *internet-working* distributes and integrates consciousness from individuals to organizations. The network is the basis for the organization to become conscious, to think, and thereby to learn.

Knowledge deployment, sometimes called knowledge management, is the creation, protection, development, and sharing of knowledge assets. When humans and their know-how are connected to each other we create a network of knowledge. The value of human capital is enhanced manifoldly by connecting organization members.

Open source both encourages learning and experimentation, and in turn benefits from it. Open source software is widespread in educational institutions, since access to the source code makes it an ideal tool for teaching. And indeed much open source software began as a learning exercise.

Learning is an ongoing journey, where both people and companies look for faster and more effective routes to personal and commercial competency. People are hired to do a job, not to spend their time being trained. However, high-performance teams do not emerge automatically, nor does leadership. Free sharing of experience is a vital ingredient for an organization to be effective.

Pedagogical research shows that communication, commitment, pleasure, social relations, and feedback are fundamental ingredients for learning. To create permanent knowledge it is essential to absorb the whole individual, and build a creative work environment as well as an organization that constantly is informing itself; that is, work characterized after the open source mind model.

The Internet age is not just an age of smart machines, but of humans who through networks can combine their intelligence, knowledge, and creativity for breakthroughs in the creation of wealth and social development.

The Five Open Source Commandments

The five open source commandments are:

➤ Care about the problem

➤ Release something useful

➤ Keep the project goals clear

➤ Facilitate steady growth

➤ Join a project rather than starting your own

First you must have a user community committed to keeping it alive. But no project starts out with dedicated members from day one. The code or work has to be reasonably stable and actually have a value—do something useful or contain some information of value—before members will even take the time to bother. For a program it must reliably solve a significant part of the problem. Then others can improve the platform.

The Netscape Navigator project described in Chapter 3, "The Open Source Philosophy," is actually a good example of a failed good intention. The source code to their Netscape Navigator was released at Mozilla.org on March 1998, but the initial release was not running code. Alas, interest from users has faded away. So far it has not created any Web browser at all. (There are other useful products from www.mozilla.org like Bugzilla, but that's another story.)

Open source software is written because someone wants to see a certain problem solved, not to make commercial software. Therefore, the project goals must be kept in clear view. Also to keep the members interested, steady progress must be made; otherwise, people lose interest and move onto another project that has more potential. They must care about the problem.

If you only have an idea or don't have a fairly stable code, look into joining a project under way rather than starting your own. There are many newsgroups, mailing lists, and Web sites for various problems. Most of them are software, but there are others. Some good generic resources are Freshmeat (www.freshmeat.net), a Web site specializing in announcing new open source software; the Ask Slashdot archives (http://slashdot.org); the Free Software Foundation's software links (www.gnu.org/software); and SourceForge (http://sourceforge.net), a clearinghouse for open source projects.

Social Aspects of Open Source

We also have found an interesting social aspect of open source we like to share. Due to low start-up costs and rapid change, open source software development offers a possible way for the developing countries to build high-value industries, leapfrogging older technologies and even modes of production.

Open source software lends itself to collaborative, community-based development at all scales from cottage industry to worldwide efforts involving the collaboration of thousands of people. Internet access potentially offers the poor the ability to communicate directly with the rest of the world, to directly present their own ideas and perspectives. Combined with the open source software development model, it allows them to participate in creating and molding the technologies and systems that will determine their future.

UNESCO (United Nations Educational, Scientific, and Cultural Organization) recognizes the social effects of open source. One of its goals is to redefine the meaning of "universal access to information" and to see how this new definition affects other aspects of modern society, such as freedom of expression, freedom of access to information, democracy, cultural identity and diversity, and the empowerment of developing economies.

UNESCO believes the Internet's penetration in society will lead to increased democratic participation in all societies and greater communication, understanding, and tolerance among people worldwide. But there is a real danger that the Internet will increase the gap between developing and developed countries and between those who have access to information and those who do not. USESCO fears that high technology and the marketplace may outrun social justice.

In a paper presented at the XXXIII International Conference of the Round Table on Archives in Stockholm, Sweden (September 9–12, 1998), Philippe Quéau, Director of Information and Informatics Division UNESCO, noted that:

> Technological standards and privacy issues, for example, are too important to be entrusted to the marketplace alone. Competing software firms have little interest in

preserving the open standards that are essential to a fully functioning interactive network. Markets encourage innovation, but they do not necessarily take account of public interest or the public good. Governments could decide to encourage and support the development of public domain software and freewares (such as LINUX, Apache). This goal may well appear absolutely vital in a few years, when the importance of equipping schools with basic computer facilities will become apparent. If we don't want to pay a global tax to Microsoft, all public sector computers should be using public domain software.

The flourishing Indian and Mexican software industry provides another obvious example. Open source software can typically be obtained for the cost of the media, typically a few dollars for a CD, or via the Internet. It can always be freely distributed. The pragmatic benefits of this are obvious. It can also take on political significance.

Mexico's Scholar Net is a program that aims to bring computers and the Net to every elementary and mid-level school in Mexico. The Mexican government expects to install from 20,000 to 35,000 labs per year for a total of 140,000 centers. Due to matters of cost, reliability, and configurability, they plan to use GNU/Linux to replace the Microsoft Windows servers. What will happen in a few years time when all these Mexican IT students enter the labor market educated in Linux and open source thinking?

India is one of the poorest countries in the world, with a large number of awfully bright, poor people. In India today, the entry-level programmer (C knowledge, but no work experience) earns a tenth of the salary of Western countries. Home PCs are not common, but with cheap entry-level computers and the price tag of $0 for software, there is an interesting new paradigm.

The new century will challenge easy classification of industries, enterprise functions, job titles, and job responsibilities.

The world became smaller a hundred years ago. The public rapidly gained access to new and dramatically faster communication technologies. Entrepreneurs, able to draw on an unprecedented scale of economics, built vast empires. Great fortunes were made. The government demanded that these powerful new monopolists be held accountable under antitrust law. Every day brought forth new technological advances to which the old business models seemed to no longer apply. Yet, somehow, the basic laws of economics asserted themselves. Those who mastered these laws survived in the new environment. Those who did not, failed.

Using the infrastructure of the emerging electricity and telephone networks, these industrialists transformed the U.S. economy, just as today's Silicon Valley entrepreneurs are drawing on computer and communications infrastructure to transform the world's economy.

Old economic principles can guide you in today's frenetic business environment. Technology changes. Economic laws do not. If you are struggling to comprehend what the Internet means for you and your business, you can learn a great deal from the advent of the century-old telephone system.

Just as the past century marked an end to easy moral, social, and cultural distinctions, so will the new century be an age of fluid and dynamic enterprise structures, in organizations, product lines, and revenue channels.

A new type of capitalism is developing, characterized by globalization of various core functions, organizational flexibility, and more authority for corporate management, entrepreneurs, and innovators at the expense of the traditional employed workforce. This makes historically unique productivity opportunities available. This new economy would be unthinkable without information technology. It also demands new ways of cooperating, like open source.

It is important to realize that the Internet did not create this trend, though it does accentuate it.

Index